Adobe® Creative Suite
Keyboard Shortcuts

Guy Hart-Davis

McGraw-Hill/Osborne
New York Chicago San Francisco
Lisbon London Madrid Mexico City
Milan New Delhi San Juan
Seoul Singapore Sydney Toronto

The McGraw·Hill Companies

McGraw-Hill/Osborne
2100 Powell Street, 10th Floor
Emeryville, California 94608
U.S.A.

To arrange bulk purchase discounts for sales promotions, premiums, or fund-raisers, please contact **McGraw-Hill**/Osborne at the above address. For information on translations or book distributors outside the U.S.A., please see the International Contact Information page immediately following the index of this book.

Adobe® Creative Suite Keyboard Shortcuts

1234567890 DOC DOC 01987654

ISBN 0-07-225499-8

Publisher	**Copy Editor**
Brandon A. Nordin	Judith Brown
Vice President &	**Proofreader**
Associate Publisher	Beatrice Wikander
Scott Rogers	**Indexer**
Editorial Director	Claire Splan
Roger Stewart	**Composition**
Project Editor	Dick Schwartz,
Madhu Prasher	Elizabeth Jang
Acquisitions Coordinator	**Illustrators**
Agatha Kim	Kathleen Edwards,
Technical Editors	Melinda Lytle
Marcia Best, Bonnie Blake,	**Series Design**
David Karlins, Doug Sahlin	Dick Schwartz,
	Peter Hancik

This book was composed with Corel VENTURA™ Publisher.

Contents

Need to get your work done faster and with less effort in the Adobe Creative Suite applications? Then use the keyboard as much as you can.

The mouse (or an equivalent, such as a drawing tablet) is great for precise graphical operations, but for invoking commands quickly and accurately, the keyboard rules. This book shows you how to make the most of your keyboard by using the hundreds of keyboard shortcuts built into the Creative Suite applications—and by creating your own keyboard shortcuts to supplement them.

Who Is This Book For?

This book is for users of the Adobe Creative Suite applications—Photoshop, Illustrator, Acrobat, InDesign, and GoLive—who want to get their work done more quickly, accurately, and efficiently on Windows, on Mac OS X, or on both platforms. If you're reading this, that probably means *you*. Unless you find yourself spending large chunks of your workday staring into space or drumming your fingers to the latest beats while waiting for more work to show up, you can benefit from saving time and effort by using keyboard shortcuts.

This book assumes that you're familiar with at least the basics of the applications you're using, and that you want to use the applications more efficiently. For example, this book assumes that you know how to start your computer, log on to the operating system, run your applications, and perform basic file management. Similarly, this book doesn't tell you what Photoshop *does* or what a PDF *is*, but rather how to work in Photoshop (and the other applications), and how to create and manipulate PDFs (and other document types), faster and more efficiently.

What Does This Book Cover?

This book explains how to use keyboard shortcuts in the Adobe Creative Suite applications running on both Windows and Mac OS X. The book presents the keyboard shortcuts arranged by application and by topic, showing screens from each platform. Within each topic, you'll learn the keyboard shortcuts you need in order to perform essential actions swiftly without reaching for your mouse.

Conventions Used in This Book

This book uses the following conventions to make the text easy to follow:

- Key caps such as 🖰-Break represent keyboard shortcuts. Hyphens mean that you should press the keys in combination.

- Multiple key caps in sequence separated by commas (for example, Ctrl-F6, Shift-F6) indicate shortcuts that are alternatives to each other. To indicate a sequence, this book uses the word "then": for example, Ctrl-Esc, then R.

Keyboard shortcuts for Windows are preceded by *Windows*, and keyboard shortcuts for the Mac are preceded by *Mac*—for example:

Windows Ctrl-N, *Mac* ⌘-N

- The ⌘ key cap represents the Command key on the Mac. The symbol represents the Apple menu, the menu that appears at the left end of the Mac OS X menu bar.

- The | symbol represents making a choice from a menu. For example, "choose File | Print" means that you should open the File menu and choose the Print command from it. (Usually, you'll press ⌘-P or Ctrl-P instead, because it's quicker.)

Keyboard Basics—and How to Enhance Your Keyboard

You'd be hard put to find a computer user who doesn't know what a keyboard is, but it would probably be nearly as difficult to find a computer user who uses the keyboard to the max. This chapter shows you how to configure your keyboard as well as possible and use such accessibility options as may help you. The chapter starts by making sure you know your way around your keyboard and the correct way to press keyboard shortcuts. After all, there's no point in getting the basics wrong.

Understanding the Standard Keys on a PC Keyboard

A standard PC keyboard (Figure 1-1) contains 101 or 104 keys that break down as follows:

- Twenty-six letter keys for the letters a through z.
- A [Spacebar] to put spaces between characters.
- Two sets of keys for the single-digit numbers (0 through 9), one set appearing as a row above the letter keys and one set on the numeric keypad. The row of

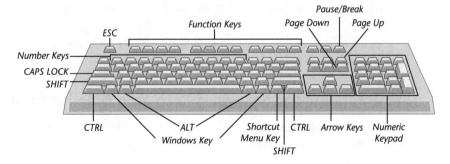

Figure 1-1   *A standard 104-key keyboard layout for PCs*

number keys double as symbol keys, and the numeric keypad keys double as navigation keys.

- Fifteen to 18 keys for mainstream punctuation symbols (for example, comma, period, and semicolon) and other symbols (for example, + and ~). The numeric keypad typically includes symbols used for basic mathematical operations (+ for addition, - for subtraction, / for division, and * for multiplication) and a period for a decimal place.

- A (Tab) key for entering tabs and for navigating from one interface element to another.

- Two (Enter) keys for entering carriage returns and "clicking" the selected button in dialog boxes.

- Two (Shift) keys to change the case of the key pressed, and a (Caps Lock) key to lock the letter keys in the capital position.

- Six other modifier keys: two (Ctrl), two (Alt), and two (⊞) (discussed in the next section).

- An (Insert) key for toggling Insert mode.

- A (Delete) key for deleting the selection or the character after the insertion point, and a (Backspace) key for deleting the character before the insertion point.

- Eight or more navigation keys: four arrow keys ((←), (→), (↑), and (↓)), a (Home) key for moving to the beginning of an item, an (End) key for moving to the end of an item, a (Page Up) key for moving up by a "page" of information, and a (Page Down) key for moving down by a page.

- Twelve function keys, numbered (F1) to (F12), for invoking functionality built into the operating system and into applications.

- A (Scroll Lock) key that toggles the locking on the scrolling function.

- A (Num Lock) key for locking on the numeric keypad.

- A (Print Screen) (or (PrtScr)) key for capturing what appears on screen.

- A (Pause/Break) key for special functions.

- An (Esc) key for canceling an action or "clicking" the Cancel button in a dialog box.

- A context menu key (or shortcut menu key) for displaying the context menu or shortcut menu.

Understanding the Standard Keys on a Mac Keyboard

Most keyboards for desktop Macs contain between 101 and 115 keys that break down as follows. Figure 1-2 shows an example of a fairly typical Mac keyboard.

- Twenty-six letter keys for the letters a through z.

- A (Spacebar) to put spaces between characters.

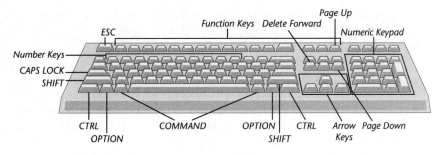

Figure 1-2 *A fairly typical Mac keyboard layout*

- Two sets of keys for the single-digit numbers (0 through 9), one set appearing as a row above the letter keys and one set on the numeric keypad. The row of number keys double as symbol keys.

- Fifteen to 18 keys for mainstream punctuation symbols (for example, comma, period, and semicolon) and other symbols (for example, + and ~). The numeric keypad typically includes symbols used for basic mathematical operations (+ for addition, - for subtraction, / for division, and * for multiplication) and a period for a decimal place.

- A Tab key for entering tabs and for navigating from one interface element to another.

- A Return key and an Enter key (on the numeric keypad) for entering carriage returns and "clicking" the selected button in dialog boxes.

- Two Shift keys to change the case of the key pressed, and a CapsLock key to lock the letter keys in the capital position.

- Six modifier keys: two Ctrl or Control keys, two Alt/Option keys, and two ⌘ keys (discussed in the next section).

- A DeleteForward key for deleting the selection or the character after the insertion point, and a Delete key for deleting the character before the insertion point.

- Eight or more navigation keys: four arrow keys (←, →, ↑, and ↓), a Home key for moving to the beginning of an item, an End key for moving to the end of an item, a PageUp key for moving up by a "page" of information, and a PageDown key for moving down by a page.

- Twelve or more function keys, numbered F1 to F12 or the appropriate higher number, for invoking functionality built into the operating system and into applications. Some keyboards have 16 function keys.

- A NumLock key for locking on the numeric keypad.

- An Esc key for canceling an action or "clicking" the Cancel button in a dialog box.

Some keyboards have extra keys for increasing and decreasing the playback volume, for toggling muting of all sound, and for ejecting the selected CD or other medium.

Using the Modifier Keys

The standard keys discussed in the previous two sections are mostly easy enough to use: to get an *a*, you press the Ⓐ key; to get a 1, you press the ① key; and so on. To use a keyboard shortcut, you typically press one of the *modifier keys*—keys that modify the effect of the key you press. (That sentence says "typically" because some keyboard shortcuts don't use any modifier key, as you'll see later in this book.)

Using the Modifier Keys in Windows

Standard keyboards for Windows PCs include four modifier keys (Figure 1-3):

- Shift   The Shift key derives from the typewriter and changes the case of the letter. The name comes from the Shift key on a typewriter physically shifting the typewriter mechanism—either lifting the platen or lowering the typebars so that the top part of the typebar (containing the uppercase letter), rather than the lower part of the typebar (containing the lowercase letter), strikes the platen. (The *typebars* are the metal bars containing the letters. The *platen* is the roller around which the sheet of paper is wrapped and fed, and against which the typebars strike.)

- Alt   The Alt key alters the keypress. In Windows, Alt is used to access accelerator keys on menus and other command bars (such as toolbars). For example, to display the File menu in many applications, you press Alt-Ⓕ.

- Ctrl   The Ctrl key (pronounced "control") is used in Windows to trigger keyboard shortcuts. For example, to issue a Print command in many applications, you can press Ctrl-Ⓟ.

- 🪟   The 🪟 is used for shortcuts that involve Windows itself rather than the applications that run on it. For example, you can press 🪟-Ⓡ to display the Run dialog box or 🪟-Break to display the System Properties dialog box.

Figure 1-3
Standard PC keyboards have four modifier keys: Shift, Alt, Ctrl, *and* 🪟.

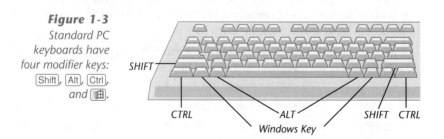

SHIFT

CTRL   ALT   SHIFT   CTRL
       Windows Key

⸢Ctrl⸥, ⸢Alt⸥, and ⸢Shift⸥ can be used in combination, thus producing many more key combinations—for example, ⸢Ctrl⸥-⸢M⸥, ⸢Ctrl⸥-⸢Alt⸥-⸢M⸥, ⸢Ctrl⸥-⸢Alt⸥-⸢Shift⸥-⸢M⸥, ⸢Ctrl⸥-⸢Shift⸥-⸢M⸥, and ⸢Alt⸥-⸢Shift⸥-⸢M⸥. The more keys in a combination, the harder it is for most users to press, but the less chance that any user will press that combination by accident. ⸢⊞⸥ isn't normally used in combination with other modifier keys, although it is possible to program Windows to recognize such key combinations.

Many laptops include another modifier key on their keyboard: the function (⸢Fn⸥) key, which is typically used to provide additional functionality on a keyboard that doesn't have enough keys for each separate function. For example, pressing ⸢Fn⸥-⸢F5⸥ on some laptops decreases the screen brightness, and ⸢Fn⸥-⸢F6⸥ increases it.

A laptop keyboard may also have an embedded keypad to provide the functionality of the keypad on a full-size keyboard. The embedded keypad usually appears on the right side of the keyboard, with the letter ⸢J⸥ doubling for ⸢1⸥, ⸢K⸥ for ⸢2⸥, and ⸢L⸥ for ⸢3⸥. You press a numeric lock key (⸢Num Lock⸥) to activate the keypad function.

Using the Modifier Keys on the Mac

Standard keyboards for Macs include four modifier keys (Figure 1-4):

- ⸢Shift⸥   The ⸢Shift⸥ key derives from the typewriter and changes the case of the letter. The name comes from the ⸢Shift⸥ key on a typewriter physically shifting the typewriter mechanism—either lifting the platen or lowering the typebars so that the top part of the typebar (containing the uppercase letter), rather than the lower part of the typebar (containing the lowercase letter), strikes the platen. (The *typebars* are the metal bars containing the letters. The *platen* is the roller around which the sheet of paper is wrapped and fed, and against which the typebars strike.)

- ⸢⌘⸥   The ⸢⌘⸥ key (the key with the Apple logo) is used in Mac OS X to trigger keyboard shortcuts. For example, to issue a Print command in many applications, you can press ⸢⌘⸥-⸢P⸥. Mac OS X uses many ⸢⌘⸥-⸢Shift⸥ shortcuts.

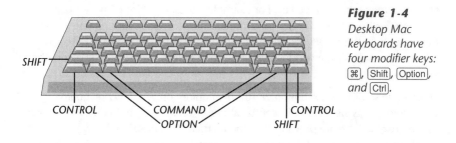

Figure 1-4
Desktop Mac keyboards have four modifier keys: ⸢⌘⸥, ⸢Shift⸥, ⸢Option⸥, *and* ⸢Ctrl⸥.

For example, pressing ⌘-Shift-A with the Finder active displays your Applications folder.

- Alt/Option   The Alt/Option key alters the keypress. For example, Photoshop uses ⌘-Option-W for the File | Close All command and ⌘-W for the File | Close command.

>> **Note:** *This book refers to the Mac* Alt/Option *key as* Option *from here on.*

- Ctrl   The Ctrl key (pronounced "control" and sometimes spelled out as Control) is used both to trigger keyboard shortcuts and to produce a right click with a single-button mouse (you hold down Ctrl while you click).

⌘, Ctrl, Option, and Shift can be used in combination, thus producing many more key combinations—for example, ⌘-M, ⌘-Option-M, ⌘-Option-Shift-M, ⌘-Shift-M, Option-M, and Option-Shift-M. The more keys in a combination, the harder it is for most users to press, but the less chance that any user will press that combination by accident.

PowerBooks and iBooks include another modifier key on their keyboard: the function (Fn) key, which is typically used to provide additional functionality on a keyboard that doesn't have enough keys for each separate function. For example, on current PowerBook models, you must press Fn and the function key to invoke the function key, because the key's primary mapping is to a hardware function: on G4 PowerBooks, the F1 key without Fn pressed decreases the screen's brightness, the F2 key without Fn pressed increases the brightness, the F3 key without Fn pressed mutes the sound, and so on.

PowerBooks and iBooks also have an embedded keypad to provide the functionality of the keypad on a full-size keyboard. The embedded keypad appears on the right side of the keyboard, with the letter J doubling for 1, K for 2, and L for 3. You press NumLock to activate the keypad function.

Pressing Key Combinations

To use a key combination, you typically hold down the modifier key or keys while you press the alphanumeric key. For example, to issue a Print command on Windows keyboards, you press Ctrl and hold it down, press and release P, and then release Ctrl. Similarly, on the Mac, you can use the ⌘-Shift-A shortcut to select all the objects in a window: you press and hold down ⌘ and Shift together while you press A.

There's one significant exception worth mentioning: on Windows keyboards, Alt works this way as well, either in combinations or on its own, but you can also press Alt and release it before pressing the alphanumeric key. Pressing the Alt key makes Windows put the focus on the first item in the menu bar, which is typically the File menu. When you press the *access key* (the underlined letter), Windows activates that menu. For example, when you press W after pressing Alt, Windows activates the <u>W</u>indow menu in many applications.

Once the menu is open, you can invoke a command on it by pressing the command's access key without pressing Alt again. In many applications, most of the frequently used commands have access keys. But because each access key needs to be unique for best effect, some less frequently used commands have either no access key or an unintuitive access key.

Access keys are also known as *mnemonics* because they frequently use the beginning letter or a key letter of the command. For example, the access key for the Save command on the File menu in standard Windows applications is *S* (the first letter), and the access key for the Exit command is *X* (the first sound in the word *exit*).

If two or more commands on the same menu use the same access key, press the key once to select the first command; then press again to select the next command. When you've reached the command you want, press Enter to invoke it. Figure 1-5 illustrates this process.

Configuring Your Keyboard in Windows

Windows XP ships with default keyboard settings that work tolerably well for many people. But to get the best results from your keyboard, you may need to configure it.

Windows XP supports three different types of configuration settings:

- **Basic keyboard settings** You can configure the speed and delay for repeating characters, and the speed at which the cursor (the insertion point) blinks.

- **Keyboard layouts** You can change the logical layout of your physical keyboard to one of a number of alternative layouts. See "Using Alternative Keyboard Layouts," later in this chapter.

Figure 1-5   *Using an* Alt *keyboard shortcut most effectively: Press* Alt *to activate the first item on the menu bar (left), press the access key to display the menu (right), and then press the access key for the command.*

- **Accessibility features**   You can use special accessibility features that Windows XP offers to make your keyboard easier to use.

If these three types of configuration settings don't give you the results you need, you may want to get a different keyboard. Many different types of keyboards are available, from ones with modest changes to the standard design to ones barely recognizable as keyboards at all.

Changing Basic Windows Keyboard Settings

Your first option is to change the rate at which the cursor blinks and the rate at which Windows XP repeats characters when you keep a key pressed down. To configure these options, choose Start | Control Panel | Printers And Other Hardware | Keyboard, and work in the Keyboard Properties dialog box (Figure 1-6).

>> Note: *If you're using Classic view of Control Panel rather than Category view, choose Start | Control Panel, and then double-click the Keyboard icon. To switch between Category view and Classic view, click the Switch To Classic View link or the Switch To Category View link in the Control Panel task pane.*

Using Windows' Keyboard Accessibility Features

If you find it difficult to press key combinations consistently, you may be able to improve matters by using Windows' keyboard accessibility features. These features

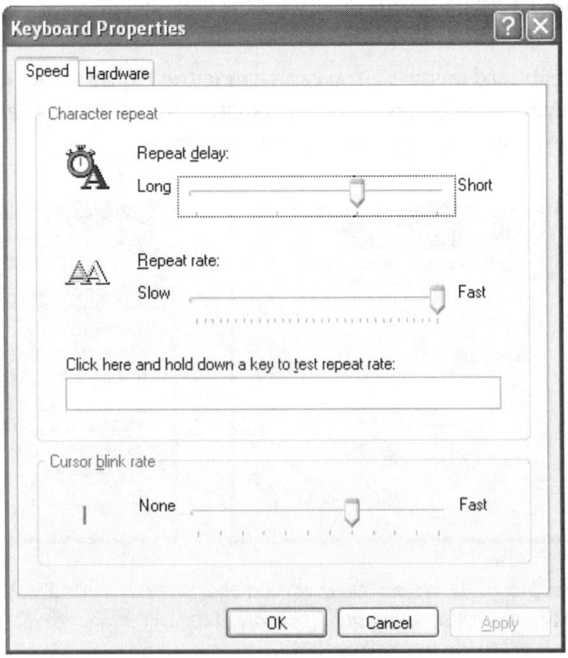

Figure 1-6
You can change your keyboard repeat rate and the cursor blink rate in the Keyboard Properties dialog box.

are designed to help Windows users who have mild to moderate disabilities, but no disability is required—if you're able-bodied, and you find an accessibility feature useful, go ahead and use it. It's not like parking in a Disabled space.

Choose Start | Control Panel to open a Control Panel window, and then click the Accessibility Options icon to display the Accessibility Options screen. Click the Accessibility Options icon again to display the Accessibility Options dialog box. If the Keyboard tab (Figure 1-7) isn't displayed, click the tab to display its controls.

The Keyboard tab offers three keyboard enhancements: StickyKeys, FilterKeys, and ToggleKeys. You can turn these enhancements on or off by selecting or clearing the Use StickyKeys check box, the Use FilterKeys check box, and the Use ToggleKeys check box on the Keyboard tab of the Accessibility Options dialog box. Each of the enhancements has configuration options that you can set by clicking the Settings button in its area and working in the resulting Settings dialog box. Most of the Settings dialog boxes offer a test area so that you can see how the current settings suit you.

StickyKeys

 StickyKeys enables you to "stick" the modifier keys on so that you can press them one at a time (for example, Alt, then Shift, then F1) instead of having to press them all together. To turn StickyKeys on, you press Shift five times in succession. To turn StickyKeys off, double-click the StickyKeys icon in the notification area to display the Accessibility Options dialog box, clear the Use StickyKeys check

Figure 1-7
*Windows'
StickyKeys,
FilterKeys, and
ToggleKeys
options can make
keyboard shortcuts
easier to press
consistently.*

Keyboard Basics *(vertical tab)*

box, and then click the OK button. (If you turn off the StickyKeys notification area icon, display the Accessibility Options dialog box from Control Panel.)

StickyKeys offers the following configuration options in its Settings For StickyKeys dialog box (Figure 1-8):

- **Use Shortcut check box**   Controls whether you can turn StickyKeys on by pressing [Shift] five times in succession.

- **Press Modifier Key Twice To Lock check box**   Controls whether Windows locks the modifier key on when you press it twice in succession. For example, press [Ctrl] twice to lock it on so that you can invoke two or more [Ctrl] keyboard shortcuts without pressing [Ctrl]. Press the same modifier key again to unlock it.

- **Turn StickyKeys Off If Two Keys Are Pressed At Once check box**   Controls whether Windows turns StickyKeys off when someone presses two keys together—in other words, when someone invokes a keyboard shortcut the normal way. This option, which is turned on by default, is intended to make StickyKeys turn off when someone who doesn't need StickyKeys starts using the computer. If you don't know that a computer is using StickyKeys, you may think it's acting very strangely.

- **Make Sounds When Modifier Key Is Pressed check box**   Controls whether Windows plays a sound when you press a modifier key. This aural feedback can be helpful if you have trouble pressing keys accurately.

- **Show StickyKeys Status On Screen check box**   Controls whether StickyKeys displays a notification-area icon to indicate that it is running. This check box is selected by default, and the reminder icon is usually helpful.

Figure 1-8
Configure StickyKeys' behavior in the Settings For StickyKeys dialog box.

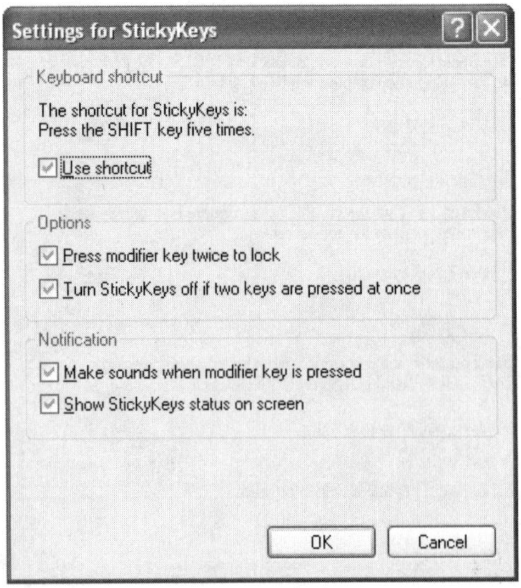

FilterKeys

FilterKeys analyzes the keystrokes that Windows experiences and tries to determine which of them are unintentional—for example, if you've entered multiple instances of the same letter in sequence by holding down a key longer than you needed to, or if you blipped the corner of a key while trying to strike another key.

FilterKeys offers the following configuration options in its Settings For FilterKeys dialog box (shown on the left in Figure 1-9):

- **Use Shortcut check box**   Controls whether you can turn on FilterKeys by holding down (Shift) for eight seconds.

- **Filter Options area**   Select the Ignore Repeated Keystrokes option button or the Ignore Quick Keystrokes And Slow Down The Repeat Rate option button, as appropriate. If you select the Ignore Repeated Keystrokes option button, click the Settings button and specify the minimum keystroke interval (from 0.5 second to 2 seconds) in the Advanced Settings For FilterKeys dialog box. If you select the Ignore Quick Keystrokes And Slow Down The Repeat Rate option button, click the Settings button and choose RepeatKeys (repeating keys) and SlowKeys (minimum-length keypresses) in the Advanced Settings For FilterKeys dialog box (shown on the right in Figure 1-9).

- **Notification area**   By default, both the Beep When Keys Pressed Or Accepted check box and the Show FilterKey Status On Screen check box are selected. Clear these check boxes if you don't find the feedback helpful. As with StickyKeys, a visual reminder tends to be useful because a computer with

Figure 1-9   *FilterKeys (left) filters out repeated and misstruck keystrokes from your typing. Use the Advanced Settings For FilterKeys dialog box (right) to configure settings for ignoring quick keystrokes and slowing down the keyboard repeat rate.*

FilterKeys active can appear to be acting very strangely—for example, you can type whole sentences and not register a single key if you're not holding down the keys long enough for SlowKeys.

ToggleKeys

ToggleKeys makes Windows play tones when you press [Caps Lock], [Num Lock], or [Scroll Lock]. ToggleKeys can be useful even for full-speed typists who may strike these keys by accident as they go for other keys. Some advanced keyboards also play warning tones to let you know that you've pressed these keys.

The only configuration option for ToggleKeys is the Use Shortcut check box, which controls whether you can turn ToggleKeys on from the keyboard by holding down [Num Lock] for five seconds.

》 Tip: *If you want to use your keyboard as much as possible, another accessibility option to try is MouseKeys, which lets you control the mouse by using the arrow keys on your keyboard. MouseKeys don't suit everybody: some people find them too slow and clumsy to be worth using. To turn on MouseKeys, choose Start | Control Panel, click the Accessibility Options link on the first screen, and then click the Accessibility Options link on the second screen to display the Accessibility Options dialog box. On the Mouse tab, select the Use MouseKeys check box. You can tune the MouseKeys settings by clicking the Settings button and working in the Settings For MouseKeys dialog box.*

Configuring Your Keyboard in Mac OS X

Like Windows, Mac OS X ships with default keyboard settings that are more or less okay for many people. But if you want to get the best results from your keyboard, you may need to configure it.

Mac OS X supports three different types of configuration settings:

- **Basic keyboard settings**   You can configure the speed and delay for repeating characters, and the speed at which the cursor (the insertion point) blinks. If you have a PowerBook with an illuminated keyboard, you can specify when to use the illumination.

- **Universal Access features**   You can use special accessibility features that Mac OS X offers to make your keyboard easier to use.

- **Keyboard layouts**   You can change the logical layout of your physical keyboard to one of a number of alternative layouts. The next main section discusses these.

》 Note: *If these three types of configuration settings don't give you the results you need, you may want to get a different keyboard. An ergonomic or specialized keyboard can make a huge difference to your comfort.*

Changing Basic Keyboard Settings on the Mac

Your first option is to change the rate at which the cursor blinks and the rate at which Mac OS X repeats characters when you keep a key pressed down. To configure these options, choose | System Preferences to display the System Preferences window, and then click the Keyboard & Mouse icon to display the Keyboard & Mouse sheet. If necessary, click the Keyboard tab to display its contents (Figure 1-10).

Drag the Key Repeat Rate slider and the Delay Until Repeat slider to suitable positions. Type in the Type Here To Test Settings box to make sure the resulting repeat rate works for you.

Press ⌘-Q or choose System Preferences | Quit System Preferences to close System Preferences.

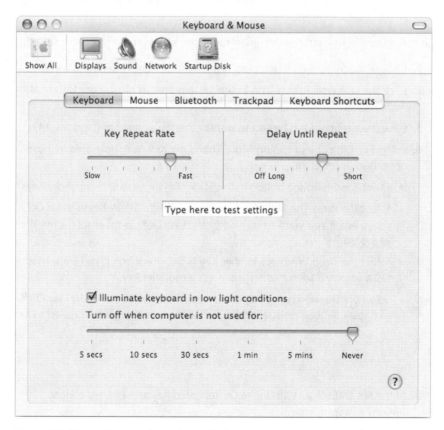

Figure 1-10 *You can change your keyboard repeat rate and delay on the Keyboard tab of the Keyboard & Mouse sheet in System Preferences.*

Using the Keyboard Universal Access Features on the Mac

If you find it difficult to press keys or key combinations consistently, you may be able to improve matters by using Mac OS X's Universal Access features. These features are designed to help users who have mild to moderate disabilities, but no disability is required—if you're able-bodied, and you find an accessibility feature useful, go ahead and use it.

There are two main Universal Access features for the keyboard:

- Sticky Keys enables you to "stick" the modifier keys on so that you can press them one at a time (for example, ⌘, then Shift, then A) instead of having to press them all together.

- Slow Keys lets you tell Mac OS X to wait a moment before accepting a keypress, and to play a sound confirming the keypress. Slow Keys is good if you find yourself triggering keys accidentally by pressing them while trying to press another key.

To configure the Universal Access features for the keyboard, follow these steps:

1. Choose ⌘ | System Preferences to display the System Preferences window.

2. Click the Universal Access icon in the System area to display the Universal Access sheet.

3. Click the Keyboard tab button to display the tab's contents (Figure 1-11).

4. In the For Difficulties Pressing More Than One Key At A Time area, choose options as appropriate:

   - Select the On option button in the Sticky Keys area to turn on Sticky Keys.

   - Select the Press The Shift Key Five Times To Turn Sticky Keys On Or Off check box if you want to be able to turn Sticky Keys on and off from the keyboard.

   - Select the Beep When A Modifier Key Is Set check box if you want Mac OS X to play a sound when you press a modifier key.

   - Select the Display Pressed Keys On Screen check box if you want Mac OS X to display symbols on screen for the modifier keys that you've pressed so far:

5. In the For Difficulties With Initial Or Repeated Keystrokes area, choose options as appropriate:

   - Select the On option button in the Slow Keys area to turn on Slow Keys.

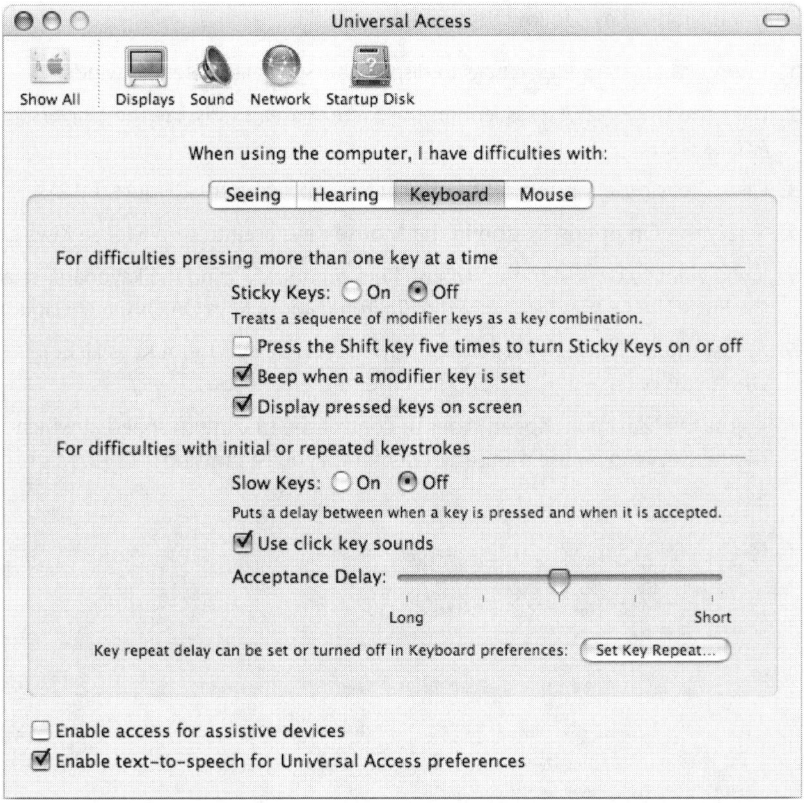

Figure 1-11   *Mac OS X's Universal Access features can make your keyboard easier to use.*

- Select the Use Click Key Sounds check box if you want Mac OS X to play a click sound to confirm each key you press. (The effect of this sound is a bit like using a typewriter.)
- Drag the Acceptance Delay slider to a suitable setting.

6. Press ⌘-Q or choose System Preferences | Quit System Preferences to close System Preferences.

Using Mouse Keys on the Mac

If you want to use your keyboard as much as possible, another accessibility option to try is Mouse Keys, which lets you control the mouse by using the arrow keys on your keyboard. Mouse Keys don't suit everybody: some people find them too slow and clumsy, but it might be worth finding out for yourself.

To turn on Mouse Keys, follow these steps:

1. Choose | System Preferences to display the System Preferences window.

2. Click the Universal Access icon in the System area to display the Universal Access sheet.

3. Click the Mouse tab button to display the tab's contents (Figure 1-12).

4. Select the On option button in the Mouse Keys area to turn Mouse Keys on.

5. If you want to be able to turn Mouse Keys on quickly using the keyboard, select the Press The Option Key Five Times To Turn Mouse Keys On Or Off check box.

6. Adjust the Initial Delay slider to control how quickly Mouse Keys kicks in when you press ←, →, ↑, or ↓ on the numeric keypad.

7. Adjust the Maximum Speed slider to control the maximum speed at which Mouse Keys moves the mouse pointer when you're pressing ←, →, ↑, or ↓.

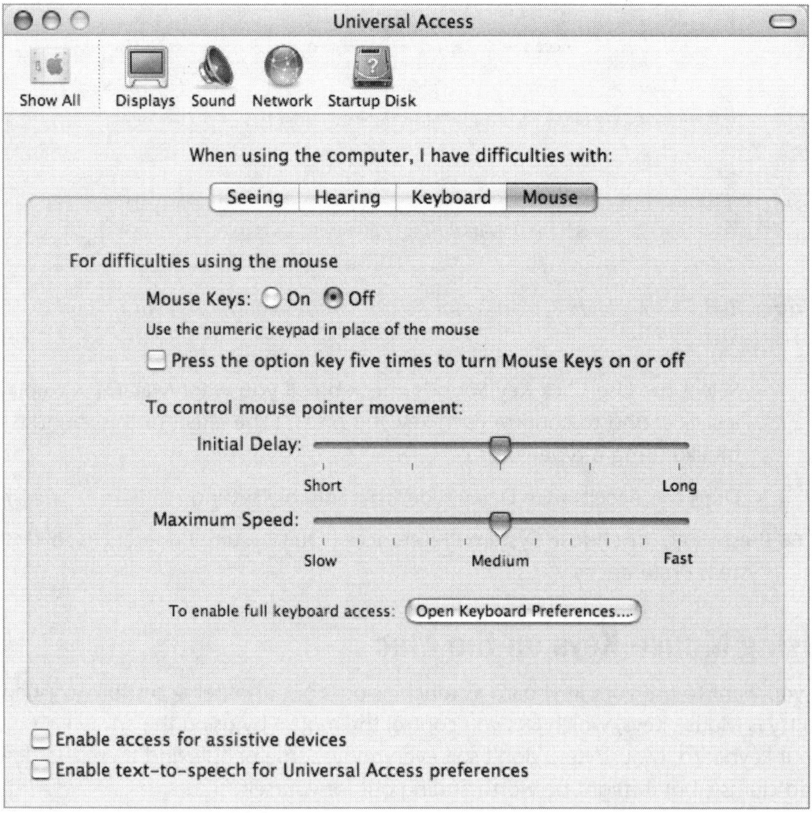

Figure 1-12   *Mac OS X's Mouse Keys feature lets you control the mouse by using the arrow keys on your keyboard.*

(Mouse Keys moves the mouse pointer slowly at first, then speeds it up to the maximum speed if you keep pressing the key.)

8. Press ⌘-Q or choose System Preferences | Quit System Preferences to close System Preferences.

Using Alternative Keyboard Layouts

The standard layout of keys on a keyboard, as you'll know from glancing at your keyboard every day, has the letters QWERTYUIOP across the top row and is generally known by the acronym QWERTY. The QWERTY layout is used almost universally in the English-typing world but isn't the most efficient or comfortable layout for extended typing.

QWERTY was designed in the 1870s by Christopher Latham Sholes, the leading inventor of the first typewriter produced in commercial quantities. The prime consideration influencing the layout was the need to prevent the keybars from jamming when the user was typing fast, but commercial considerations were also involved: Sholes included all the letters for the word *typewriter* in the top line so that his salesmen could type it more easily when demonstrating the typewriter. The result was that only about 36 percent of the letters you type on a QWERTY keyboard are on the home row, so your fingers have to move frequently to the other rows of keys.

As you'll probably agree from your experience of learning to type, the QWERTY layout isn't easy to learn; if you use it extensively, you may also agree that it's not efficient to use either. But because it became the standard layout relatively quickly after its introduction, and because it has remained the standard layout in the English-typing world, QWERTY has such a lock on the market that no alternative keyboard layout has gained much traction. Not surprisingly, few people want to learn to type again, and QWERTY works well enough once you've learned it, so it seems likely to be with us to stay.

The keyboard layout is "hard-coded" into a typewriter, so to change the letter that a key delivers, you'd need to saw the keybar off and weld on a different one. With computers, making changes is much easier. The physical layout of the keyboard is hard-coded, although with some keyboards, you can pop off the key caps (the caps that constitute the physical keys) and slide them back on in different places if you choose. (This works only for standard keyboards.) But the logical layout can be changed either on the keyboard or on the computer with minimal effort. Should you want to try a different keyboard layout, you need only tell your keyboard or your computer so.

Which Layout Should You Use?

At this point, you're probably not too excited about the possibilities of logical layouts unless you have a particular logical layout in mind. After all, to use a different layout, you either need to buy a keyboard that has that layout, physically customize your keyboard to show that layout (for example, by rearranging the key caps or pasting stickers over the letters on them), or touch-type on a keyboard whose keys show different letters than they deliver. (You should be touch-typing in any case, because doing so saves you a huge amount of time and effort over looking for the keys. But even so, having each key produce a different letter than it bears can be disconcerting, especially when you're trying to type passwords and can't see on screen which letters you're getting.)

For most people, the primary alternative is one of the implementations of the Dvorak keyboard layout—for example, the United States-Dvorak layout that comes built into Windows XP or the Dvorak layout included with Mac OS X. Unlike QWERTY, the Dvorak layout was designed for efficient typing in English, and in typical use, about 74 percent of keystrokes are on the home row, so your fingers needn't move nearly as far as with QWERTY. August Dvorak, the inventor of the Dvorak layout, also laid out the keys to use as much as possible the hand's natural drumming rhythm from pinkie to index finger.

The Dvorak layout has many enthusiasts (full disclosure: I'm one) but has barely scratched the surface of the mainstream typing market because QWERTY, as the default keyboard format, has the market pretty thoroughly sewn up. You can buy keyboards with Dvorak layouts from specialist keyboard retailers, but the easiest way to get started is to download a Dvorak key chart from the Internet, apply the Windows XP United States-Dvorak keyboard layout (using the technique discussed next) or the Mac OS X Dvorak layout (using the technique described later in this chapter), and learn to touch-type with it.

Dvorak's far from the only option: Windows XP supports an impressive array of different keyboard layouts, as does Mac OS X. But unless you learned to type on a particular keyboard layout, or a layout offers better key placement for particular keys you find difficult to press, you won't usually have a strong reason for choosing it over your existing keyboard layout.

Working with Alternative Keyboard Layouts in Windows

This section discusses how to work with the alternative keyboard layouts in Windows. You'll learn how to apply a different keyboard layout, how to switch between (or among) keyboard layouts, and how to use and configure the Language bar.

Applying a Different Keyboard Layout

To apply a different keyboard layout in Windows, follow these steps:

1. Choose Start | Control Panel to display Control Panel.

2. Click the Date, Time, Language, And Regional Options item to display the Date, Time, Language, And Regional Options screen.

3. Click the Regional And Language Options item to display the Regional And Language Options dialog box.

4. Click the Languages tab to display its contents.

5. In the Text Services And Input Languages group box, click the Details button to display the Text Services And Input Languages dialog box (Figure 1-13).

6. Click the Add button to display the Add Input Language dialog box:

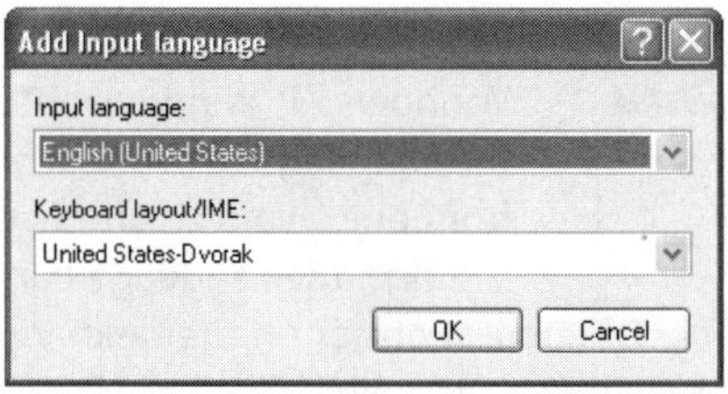

7. In the Input Language drop-down list, select the input language if necessary. (For some keyboard layouts, you can simply leave your current input language selected.)

8. In the Keyboard Layout/IME drop-down list, select the keyboard layout you want to use. For example, select the United States-Dvorak layout to use the Dvorak layout with a standard U.S. keyboard.

9. Click the OK button to close the Add Input Language dialog box and add the layout to the list in the Installed Services list box.

Figure 1-13
Use the Settings tab of the Text Services And Input Languages dialog box to add any other keyboard layouts you want to use with Windows XP.

10. Add further layouts as necessary by repeating steps 6 through 9.

11. Click the OK button to close the Text Services And Input Languages dialog box.

12. Click the OK button to close the Regional And Language Options dialog box.

13. Click the close button (the × button) to close the Date, Time, Language, And Regional Options dialog box.

Switching Among Keyboard Layouts in Windows

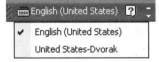

When you add a second keyboard layout to Windows XP, Windows XP automatically displays the Language bar so that you can easily switch from one layout to another. Depending on your settings, the Language bar may appear either as a free-floating bar over your applications or on the taskbar just to the left of the notification area. Either way, you can switch from one layout to another by clicking the Keyboard icon and choosing the layout from the resulting menu.

Given that we're talking about keyboard shortcuts in this book, you may prefer to switch among keyboard layouts by using keyboard shortcuts rather than the mouse. To set your computer up to do so, follow these steps:

1. Right-click the Language bar or the taskbar icon, and choose Settings from the shortcut menu to display the Text Services And Input Languages dialog box. When you display the dialog box this way, it contains only the Settings tab, but otherwise it's the same as shown in Figure 1-13, earlier in this chapter.

2. Click the Key Settings button to display the Advanced Key Settings dialog box:

3. In the Hot Keys For Input Languages group box, select the item for which you want to set the key sequence:

- This group box contains a Switch Between Input Languages item that switches to the next keyboard layout, and a Switch To item for each input language and keyboard layout—for example, "Switch to English (United States) - United States-Dvorak" for the United States-Dvorak keyboard layout using U.S. English.

- The Switch Between Input Languages item is set by default to [LeftAlt]-[Shift]. Note that [LeftAlt] is [Alt] on the left of the keyboard, not [←]-[Alt].

4. Click the Change Key Sequence button to display the Change Key Sequence dialog box:

Change Key Sequence	? X
Switch to English (United States) - United States-Dvorak	
☑ Enable Key Sequence	
○ CTRL + SHIFT + Key: 0 ⌄	OK
⊙ Left ALT	Cancel

5. Select the Enable Key Sequence check box if it's not already selected.

6. Select the CTRL option button to create a keyboard shortcut using [Ctrl]-[Shift] or the Left ALT option button to create a shortcut using [Alt]-[Shift].

7. In the Key drop-down list, select the number key to use for the keyboard shortcut. You can also select the tilde key (~) or the grave accent key (`) if you prefer.

8. Click the OK button to close the Change Key Sequence dialog box. Windows XP adds the new keyboard shortcut to the list in the Advanced Key Settings dialog box.

9. Repeat steps 3 through 8 to create keyboard shortcuts for as many of your other keyboard layouts as you want.

10. Click the OK button to close the Advanced Key Settings dialog box.

11. Click the OK button to close the Text Services And Input Languages dialog box.

You can then switch to a different keyboard layout by pressing the keyboard shortcut you chose for it. Alternatively, press the Switch Between Input Languages keyboard shortcut to cycle through your keyboard layouts.

Switching the Language Bar Between Docked and Floating

To dock the Language bar from its free-floating state, right-click it and choose Minimize from the shortcut menu. Windows XP displays a Language bar message box to make sure you know what you've done. Select the Don't Show Me This Message Again check box, and click the OK button to close the message box.

To undock the Language bar, right-click it and choose Restore The Language Bar from the shortcut menu.

Configuring How the Language Bar Appears

To configure how the Language bar appears, or to turn it off, follow these steps:

1. Right-click the Language bar or the taskbar icon and choose Settings from the shortcut menu to display the Text Services And Input Languages dialog box.

2. Click the Language Bar button to display the Language Bar Settings dialog box:

3. Choose settings as appropriate:

    - Select the Show The Language Bar On The Desktop check box to display the Language bar.

    - Select the Show The Language Bar As Transparent When Inactive check box if you want Windows to make the Language bar transparent when you're not actively using it. This check box is available only when the Language bar is floating, not when it is docked on the taskbar.

    - Select the Show Additional Language Bar Icons In The Notification Area check box if you want to display all the Language bar icons in the taskbar. (Depending on your configuration of Windows XP and Office, this check box may be called Show Additional Language Bar Icons In The Taskbar.)

    - Select the Show Text Labels On The Language Bar check box if you want to display text labels as well as icons on the Language bar. Text labels make the buttons more comprehensible, but they take up more space. This check box is available only when the Language bar is floating, not when it is docked on the taskbar.

    - Select or clear the Turn Off Advanced Text Services check box to control whether text services such as speech recognition and handwriting recognition are turned on or off. If you're not using these features, clear this check box.

4. Click the OK button to close the Language Bar Settings dialog box.

5. Click the OK button to clear the Text Services And Input Languages dialog box.

Working with Alternative Keyboard Layouts on the Mac

This section discusses how to work with the alternative keyboard layouts on the Mac. You'll learn how to apply a different keyboard layout and how to switch between (or among) keyboard layouts.

Applying a Different Keyboard Layout

To apply a different keyboard layout, follow these steps:

1. Choose | System Preferences to display the System Preferences window.

2. Click the International icon in the Personal area to display the International sheet.

3. Click the Input Menu tab button to display the Input Menu tab (Figure 1-14).

Figure 1-14   *Use the Input Menu tab of the International sheet in System Preferences to apply a different logical keyboard layout.*

4. Select the check box in the On column for each keyboard layout you want to add to the input menu. If you just want to have one layout available, make sure that its check box is the only one selected.

5. If you choose to load two or more layouts, and you want to be able to switch among them by using the mouse, make sure the Show Input Menu In Menu Bar check box is selected.

6. If you choose to load two or more layouts, and you want to be able to switch among them by using the keyboard rather than the input menu, click the Options button to display the Input Menu Shortcuts pane (shown here). Make sure the Holding Down Command + Option And Typing Space Will Step Through All Items In The Input Menu check box is selected, and then click the OK button.

Input Menu Shortcuts

Command+Space will toggle between the last two
scripts selected in the Input menu

⌘ + space

☑ Holding down Command+Option and typing Space
will step through all items in the Input menu

⌘ + option + space

☑ Try to match keyboard with text

When selecting text, try to switch to a keyboard layout or
input method appropriate to the text.

Cancel   OK

7. Press ⌘-Q or choose System Preferences | Quit System Preferences to close System Preferences.

≫ Note: *You can add keyboard layouts to those that Mac OS X provides by copying the keyboard layout file to your Mac. Put the file in /Library (your Mac's main Library folder) to make it available for every user. Put the file in your ~/Library folder (the Library folder in your Home folder) to keep it to yourself.*

Switching Among Keyboard Layouts on the Mac

When you have two or more keyboard layouts loaded, you can switch among them by using either the input menu or keyboard shortcuts:

- If you selected the Show Input Menu In Menu Bar check box on the Input Menu tab of the International sheet in System Preferences, Mac OS X displays the input menu on the menu bar. Click the input menu icon (which shows an icon for the current layout) and choose the layout from the menu:

- Press ⌘-Spacebar to toggle between the last two layouts you've used.
- Press ⌘-Option-Spacebar to select the next item in the input menu.

Using Remapping Utilities to Remap the Keys on Your Keyboard

By this point, you should have your keyboard pretty well configured. But there's one more option you should be aware of: you can remap the keys on your keyboard so that they produce different keystrokes than normal for the keyboard layout you're using.

This is where it gets a little weird. With a standard keyboard layout, such as U.S. English, you'll get the letter for the key you press: press C, you get a *c*, and so on. If you've applied a different keyboard layout, such as Dvorak, you'll get a different letter for that same key: press C, and you get a *j*, because that's where the *j* is in the Dvorak layout. But even with a different keyboard layout applied, you can remap any given key so that it produces a different keystroke yet.

Fair enough, you may be saying—but why would you want to remap a key from your chosen layout? The usual reason is to work around a marginally abnormal layout that the manufacturer has designed into your laptop. For example, for years Toshiba designed its laptop keyboards with only one Alt key, which was positioned in the regular location for the left Alt key. Anyone used to using the right Alt key was straight out of luck if they or their company bought a Toshiba laptop. But with a remapping utility, they could make the key Toshiba put in the right Alt position into an Alt key, thus saving time and temper. Similarly, some people like to swap the positions of Ctrl and CapsLock on their keys to make typing easier. Others find they want to put a ⌘ key next to a Shift key so that they can invoke keyboard shortcuts more easily on Mac OS X.

To remap the keys, you use a remapping utility. If you search on the Web, you'll find various remapping utilities—mostly for Windows, but you'll find some for the Mac as well if you search diligently. Some remappers are free, having been written by disgruntled keyboard users who choose to share the fruits of their labors. Others cost a few dollars.

At this writing, one of the best freeware remappers for Windows XP is Travis Krumsick's KeyTweak, which you can download from **http://webpages.charter .net/krumsick/**. KeyTweak has a straightforward interface in which you specify which physical key to remap, which logical key to remap it to, and then commit the changes.

Remapping Your Keyboard Physically

Logical remapping is one thing, physical remapping another. If you apply a different keyboard layout, or remap keys logically by using a remapping utility, you'll end up with keys that produce a different letter from that shown on the key caps. If you're touch-typing, that may not be too much of a problem, but you may still be tempted to improve matters.

With some keyboards, you can pop off the key caps and put them back on in different positions without doing any damage. With others, you'll find that some keys fit only in certain positions, and that you can't change the layout of the key caps physically. In this case, your best bet is to apply stickers neatly over the keys you've changed.

Cubeboard (**www.personalkeyboard.com**) has announced keyboards (and other products, such as remote controls) in which you can easily remove and rearrange the keys. Better yet, each key cap is hard-coded to its characters, so it "knows" which letter to produce; when you move the key cap to a different position on the keyboard, it still delivers the same letter, so you don't need to apply a different logical layout or remap keys.

Cubeboard's plans sound great, but at this writing, Cubeboard hasn't brought its products to market.

Photoshop Keyboard Shortcuts

In Photoshop, the mouse (or an equivalent tool) is indispensable—but that doesn't mean the keyboard shouldn't contribute as much as it can. Adobe has built into Photoshop a huge amount of keyboard functionality that many users largely ignore. By tapping into this functionality, and by customizing it to suit your needs, you can not only reduce the amount of work your mouse hand does but even get your work done faster.

As its title suggests, this chapter concentrates on keyboard shortcuts—commands you can issue by pressing keys on the keyboard. It also discusses some, but not all, of the instances when you can press one or more modifier keys to affect a mouse action, such as pressing Alt or Option to change the effect of a click or drag operation.

Opening, Closing, and Saving Files

No matter which types of work you perform in Photoshop, you'll almost certainly need to open files to work with, save the changes you make, and close the files you've finished changing. You can perform all these tasks from the keyboard.

Keyboard Shortcuts for Creating New Files and Opening Existing Files

Windows Ctrl-N, *Mac* ⌘-N

Display the New dialog box

From the New dialog box (the Mac version is shown here), you can choose the details of the new picture you're creating and assign it a name. Click the Advanced drop-down button to display the Color Profile drop-down list and the Pixel Aspect Ratio drop-down list.

Windows Ctrl-O, *Mac* ⌘-O

Display the Open dialog box

Use the Open dialog box to quickly open files whose locations and names you know.

Windows Ctrl-Shift-O, *Mac* ⌘-Shift-O

Display the File Browser

Use the File Browser to locate the files you want to open. You can use the following keyboard shortcuts to navigate and perform actions in the File Browser:

Windows	**Mac**	**Effect**
Ctrl-↑	⌘-↑	Move up a level in folder view.
F5	F5	Refresh the tree and thumbnail panes.
Ctrl-]	⌘-]	Rotate the selected thumbnail clockwise.
Ctrl-[	⌘-[	Rotate the selected thumbnail counterclockwise.
Alt-Enter	Alt-Return	Open the selected file and close the File Browser.
Shift-Enter	Shift-Return	Open the selected file, suppressing any open options or color warning dialog boxes.

Windows Ctrl-Alt-O

Display the Open As dialog box

Display the Open As dialog box instead of the Open dialog box when you need to specify the format in which to open a file. Choose the format in the Open As drop-down list. You may need to specify the format after moving or copying a file from Mac OS X to Windows or vice versa.

» Note: *On the Mac, Photoshop doesn't offer an Open As command because the Open dialog box contains a Format drop-down list that you can use to specify the format in which to open the file.*

Windows [Ctrl]-[Shift]-[M], *Mac* [⌘]-[Shift]-[M]

Open the file for editing in ImageReady

Press this shortcut (or choose File | Edit In ImageReady) to open the current file in Photoshop for editing in ImageReady. From ImageReady, you can press this shortcut to open the current file for editing in Photoshop.

Keyboard Shortcuts for Closing Files and Quitting Photoshop

Windows [Ctrl]-[W], [Ctrl]-[F4], *Mac* [⌘]-[W]

Close the active file

If the active file contains unsaved changes, Photoshop prompts you to save them.

> **» Note:** *The two Windows keyboard shortcuts shown here, [Ctrl]-[W] and [Ctrl]-[F4], are alternatives to each other, not a sequence of commands. To indicate a sequence of commands, this book uses the word then—for example, [Alt]-[·], then [N].*

Windows [Ctrl]-[Alt]-[W], *Mac* [⌘]-[Option]-[W]

Close all open files

If any of the open files contains unsaved changes, Photoshop prompts you to save them.

Windows [Ctrl]-[Q], [Alt]-[F4], *Mac* [⌘]-[Q]

Quit Photoshop

Keyboard Shortcuts for Saving Files

Windows [Ctrl]-[S], *Mac* [⌘]-[S]

Save the active file

The first time you save a file, Photoshop displays the Save As dialog box so that you can specify the filename, the folder, and the format to use. Thereafter, when you issue a Save command, Photoshop saves the file under its existing name without displaying the Save As dialog box.

Windows [Ctrl]-[Shift]-[S], *Mac* [⌘]-[Shift]-[S]

Display the Save As dialog box

Use this shortcut (or the File | Save As command) to save a previously saved file under a different name.

Photoshop

Windows Ctrl - Alt - Shift - S, *Mac* ⌘ - Option - Shift - S

Display the Save For Web dialog box

The Save For Web dialog box offers options for quickly saving the active file in a format optimized for the Web. You can click the Edit In ImageReady button to edit the file in ImageReady.

Configuring Photoshop

To make Photoshop behave the way you want it to, you'll probably need to configure some of the hundreds of options it offers in the Preferences dialog box. You may also want to change your color settings in the Color Settings dialog box and use the Keyboard Shortcuts dialog box to create custom keyboard shortcuts.

Keyboard Shortcuts for Configuring Photoshop

Windows Ctrl - K, *Mac* ⌘ - K

Display the General sheet of the Preferences dialog box

The General sheet of the Preferences dialog box is the only sheet that you can access directly with a keyboard shortcut from Photoshop. (You can access the other sheets directly from the Edit | Preferences submenu on Windows and the Photoshop | Preferences submenu on the Mac.) Once you've displayed the General sheet, you can access the other sheets by using the following keyboard shortcuts:

Windows	**Mac**	**Preferences Sheet**
Ctrl - 1	⌘ - 1	General
Ctrl - 2	⌘ - 2	File Handling
Ctrl - 3	⌘ - 3	Display & Cursors
Ctrl - 4	⌘ - 4	Transparency & Gamut
Ctrl - 5	⌘ - 5	Units & Rulers
Ctrl - 6	⌘ - 6	Guides, Grid & Slices
Ctrl - 7	⌘ - 7	Plug-Ins & Scratch Disks
Ctrl - 8	⌘ - 8	Memory & Image Cache
Ctrl - 9	⌘ - 9	File Browser

Windows Ctrl - Shift - K, *Mac* ⌘ - Shift - K

Display the Color Settings dialog box

Use the Color Settings dialog box to choose the set of color settings you want to use (for example, North America General Purpose Defaults) and make any necessary tweaks to them.

Windows Ctrl-Alt-Shift-K, *Mac* ⌘-Option-Shift-K

Display the Keyboard Shortcuts dialog box

See "Customizing Keyboard Shortcuts," later in this chapter, for a discussion of how to customize Photoshop's default keyboard shortcuts and create further shortcuts of your own.

Getting Information and Help

Photoshop provides keyboard shortcuts for getting information about the active file and for launching Photoshop Help.

Keyboard Shortcuts for Getting Information About the Active File

Windows Ctrl-Alt-I, *Mac* ⌘-Option-I

Display the information dialog box for the active file

Keyboard Shortcuts for Getting Help

Windows F1, *Mac* ⌘-/

Launch Photoshop Help

Mac OS X » F1 is used for Undo and Redo on Mac OS X.

Undoing and Redoing Actions, and Reverting

Photoshop enables you to undo the last action you've done and redo the last action you've undone. Beyond that, Photoshop enables you to *step backward* through the last actions you've taken, effectively undoing the changes you've made. After stepping backward, you can *step forward* again, effectively redoing the changes. The History palette helps you track the steps you've taken.

Keyboard Shortcuts for Undo, Redo, and Revert

Windows Ctrl-Z, *Mac* ⌘-Z, F1

Undo the last action, or redo the last undone action

Windows Ctrl-Alt-Z, *Mac* ⌘-Option-Z

Step backward

Windows Ctrl-Shift-Z, *Mac* ⌘-Shift-Z

Step forward

Windows F12, *Mac* F12

Revert to the last saved version of the file

By reverting to the last saved version of the file, you can easily discard all changes you've made to the file since you last saved it. You can achieve a similar effect by closing the file without saving changes, and then reopening it. The advantage of the Revert command, which you can issue by using this shortcut or choosing File | Revert, is that Photoshop adds the reversion to the History palette, so you can undo it if necessary.

Changing Page Setup and Printing

When you've got an image ready for printing, check the page setup, preview the picture, and then print it. You can perform these operations easily with keyboard shortcuts. You can also print an image quickly without using the Print dialog box.

Keyboard Shortcuts for Page Setup and Printing

Windows Ctrl-Shift-P, *Mac* ⌘-Shift-P

Display the Page Setup dialog box

In the Page Setup dialog box, you can choose the paper size, orientation, margins, and other options.

Windows Ctrl-Alt-P, *Mac* ⌘-Option-P

Display the Print dialog box containing a preview of the image

Use this shortcut (or choose File | Print With Preview) when you want to check how your image will look before you print it. For subsequent print operations with the same image, you may prefer to use the Print command, which doesn't show a preview.

Windows Ctrl-P, *Mac* ⌘-P

Display the Print dialog box

Windows Ctrl-Alt-Shift-P, *Mac* ⌘-Option-Shift-P

Print one copy

Press this shortcut (or choose File | Print One Copy) to print one copy of the active image with current print settings without displaying the Print dialog box.

» Tip: *In many of Photoshop's dialog boxes, you can press* Alt *(in Windows) or* Option *(on the Mac) to change the Cancel button to a Reset button for resetting the dialog box. The* Alt *or* Option *keypress may also change other buttons in the dialog box: for example, in the version of the Print dialog box that includes a preview of the image, pressing* Alt *or* Option *changes the Print button to a Print One button, the Cancel button to a Reset button, and the Done button to a Remember button. Similarly, in a dialog box such as the Filter Galley dialog box, pressing* Ctrl *(in Windows) or* ⌘ *(on the Mac) changes the Cancel button to a Default button.*

Cutting, Copying, and Pasting

In addition to the standard Windows and Mac keyboard shortcuts for Cut (*Windows* Ctrl-X, *Mac* ⌘-X), Copy (*Windows* Ctrl-C, *Mac* ⌘-C), and Paste (*Windows* Ctrl-V, *Mac* ⌘-V), Photoshop offers further keyboard shortcuts on both platforms.

Keyboard Shortcuts for Cut, Copy, and Paste

Windows F2, *Mac* F2

Cut

Windows F3, *Mac* F3

Copy

Windows F4, *Mac* F4

Paste

Windows Ctrl-Shift-V, *Mac* ⌘-Shift-V

Paste the cut or copied item inside another selection

Select the destination for the Paste Into operation before you press this shortcut or choose Edit | Paste Into.

Photoshop

Windows Ctrl - Shift - C , *Mac* ⌘ - Shift - C

Create a merged copy of the visible layers in the selection

Changing the View

Photoshop provides keyboard shortcuts for zooming the view, for working with view items, and for viewing images.

Keyboard Shortcuts for Zooming the View

Windows Ctrl - + , *Mac* ⌘ - +

Zoom in

Press this shortcut multiple times to zoom in as far as necessary.

Windows Ctrl - - , *Mac* ⌘ - -

Zoom out

Press this shortcut multiple times to zoom out as far as necessary.

Windows Ctrl - 0 , *Mac* ⌘ - 0

Zoom the image to fit on screen

The Fit On Screen command (which you can also choose from the View menu) zooms the image to the largest size at which the whole image fits on the screen. You can also invoke this command by double-clicking the Hand tool.

Windows Ctrl - Alt - 0 , *Mac* ⌘ - Option - 0

Display the image at 100 percent size

This shortcut is the equivalent of the View | Active Pixels command.

Windows Ctrl - Spacebar , *Mac* ⌘ - Spacebar

Temporarily activate the Zoom In tool

Hold down this shortcut to activate the Zoom In tool, and then click to zoom in.

Windows Alt - Spacebar , *Mac* Option - Spacebar

Temporarily activate the Zoom Out tool

Hold down this shortcut to activate the Zoom Out tool, and then click to zoom out.

Windows [Ctrl]-drag, *Mac* [⌘]-drag

Zoom in on a particular area of an image

[Ctrl]-drag (in Windows) or [⌘]-drag (on the Mac) over the area of the preview in the Navigator palette.

Keyboard Shortcuts for Working with View Items

Windows [Ctrl]-[Y], *Mac* [⌘]-[Y]

Toggle Proof Colors on and off

Windows [Ctrl]-[Shift]-[Y], *Mac* [⌘]-[Shift]-[Y]

Toggle Gamut Warning on and off

When you turn Gamut Warning on by pressing this shortcut or by choosing View | Gamut Warning, Photoshop highlights all pixels that contain out-of-gamut colors.

Windows [Ctrl]-[H], *Mac* [⌘]-[H]

Toggle the display of all extras

Extras are nonprinting items such as the grid, guides, target paths, annotations, and selection edges. Instead of turning on the display of all extras, you can turn on the display of only that extra you need.

Windows [Ctrl]-[R], *Mac* [⌘]-[R]

Toggle the display of the vertical and horizontal rulers

Windows [Ctrl]-[Shift]-[;], *Mac* [⌘]-[Shift]-[;]

Enable or disable snapping

Windows [Ctrl]-[Alt]-[;], *Mac* [⌘]-[Option]-[;]

Toggle the locking on guides

Lock guides when you want to make sure that you don't move them accidentally.

Windows [Ctrl]-[Shift]-[H], *Mac* [⌘]-[Shift]-[H]

Toggle the display of the target path

The target path displays all the anchor points, direction lines, and direction points for the selected object.

Photoshop

Windows Ctrl -' , *Mac* ⌘ -'

Toggle the display of the grid

Keyboard Shortcuts for Viewing Images

Windows Ctrl - Tab , *Mac* Ctrl - Tab

Cycle through the open images

Windows Q , *Mac* Q

Toggle between Standard Edit mode and Quick Mask mode

Windows F , *Mac* F

Switch among Standard Screen mode, Full Screen mode with menu bar, and Full Screen mode

Windows Page Up , *Mac* Page Up

Scroll up one screen

Windows Page Down , *Mac* Page Down

Scroll down one screen

Windows Shift - Page Up , *Mac* Shift - Page Up

Scroll up ten units

Windows Shift - Page Down , *Mac* Shift - Page Down

Scroll down ten units

Windows Home , *Mac* Home

Move the view to the upper-left corner of the image

Windows End , *Mac* End

Move the view to the lower-right corner of the image

Selecting and Moving Objects

To work with an object, you'll typically need to select it. Photoshop offers plenty of keyboard shortcuts for selecting and moving objects.

Keyboard Shortcuts for Selecting Items

Windows Ctrl-A, *Mac* ⌘-A

Select all items

Windows Ctrl-D, *Mac* ⌘-D

Deselect the current selection

Windows Ctrl-Shift-D, *Mac* ⌘-Shift-D

Reselect the previous selection

After deselecting a selection and realizing you still need to work with it, you can press this shortcut to reselect the selection.

Windows Ctrl-Shift-I, Shift-F7, *Mac* ⌘-Shift-I, Shift-F7

Invert the selection

Windows Spacebar-drag, *Mac* Spacebar-drag

Reposition the marquee while creating a selection

This shortcut works with any marquee tool except the Single Column Marquee tool and the Single Row Marquee tool.

Windows Shift-drag, *Mac* Shift-drag

Add to the selection

This shortcut works when any of the selection tools is active.

Windows Alt-drag, *Mac* Option-drag

Subtract from the selection

This shortcut works when any of the selection tools is active.

Windows Shift-drag, *Mac* Shift-drag

Constrain the marquee

Hold down Shift to constrain the Rectangular Marquee tool to a square and the Elliptical Marquee tool to a circle. This shortcut works when no other selections are active.

Windows Alt-drag, *Mac* Option-drag

Draw the marquee from the center

This shortcut works when no other selections are active.

Windows Alt-Shift-drag, *Mac* Option-Shift-drag

Draw a constrained marquee from the center

Hold down Shift to constrain the Rectangular Marquee tool to a square and the Elliptical Marquee tool to a circle.

Keyboard Shortcuts for Moving Objects

Windows Ctrl, *Mac* ⌘

Switch to the Move tool

This shortcut works when a tool other than the Hand tool, the Slice tool, the Path tool, the Shape tool, the Rectangle tool, or a Pen tool is selected.

Windows Alt-drag, *Mac* Option-drag

Switch from the Magnetic Lasso tool to the Lasso tool

Windows Alt-click, *Mac* Option-click

Switch from the Magnetic Lasso tool to the Polygonal Lasso tool

Windows Enter, *Mac* Return

Apply the Magnetic Lasso

This shortcut works when the Magnetic Lasso is selected.

Windows Esc, *Mac* Esc

Cancel the Magnetic Lasso

This shortcut works when the Magnetic Lasso is selected.

Windows 〔]〕 and Magnetic Lasso, *Mac* 〔]〕 and Magnetic Lasso

   Increase the detection width

Windows 〔[〕 and Magnetic Lasso, *Mac* 〔[〕 and Magnetic Lasso

   Decrease the detection width

Windows 〔Alt〕-drag with Move tool, *Mac* 〔Option〕-drag with Move tool

   Move a copy of the selection

Windows 〔←〕, 〔→〕, 〔↑〕, 〔↓〕, *Mac* 〔←〕, 〔→〕, 〔↑〕, 〔↓〕

   Move the selection area by one pixel in the direction of the arrow pressed

   This shortcut and the next move the selection area, not the selection.

Windows 〔Shift〕-〔←〕, 〔Shift〕-〔→〕, 〔Shift〕-〔↑〕, 〔Shift〕-〔↓〕,
  Mac 〔Shift〕-〔←〕, 〔Shift〕-〔→〕, 〔Shift〕-〔↑〕, 〔Shift〕-〔↓〕

   Move the selection area by ten pixels in the direction of the arrow pressed

Windows 〔←〕, 〔→〕, 〔↑〕, 〔↓〕 and Move tool, *Mac* 〔←〕, 〔→〕, 〔↑〕, 〔↓〕 and Move tool

   Move the selection by one pixel in the direction of the arrow pressed

Windows 〔Shift〕-〔←〕, 〔Shift〕-〔→〕, 〔Shift〕-〔↑〕, 〔Shift〕-〔↓〕 and Move tool,
  Mac 〔Shift〕-〔←〕, 〔Shift〕-〔→〕, 〔Shift〕-〔↑〕, 〔Shift〕-〔↓〕 and Move tool

   Move the selection by ten pixels in the direction of the arrow pressed

Windows 〔Ctrl〕-〔←〕, 〔Ctrl〕-〔→〕, 〔Ctrl〕-〔↑〕, 〔Ctrl〕-〔↓〕,
  Mac 〔⌘〕-〔←〕, 〔⌘〕-〔→〕, 〔⌘〕-〔↑〕, 〔⌘〕-〔↓〕

   Move all objects on the layer by one pixel

   This shortcut works only when there is no selection on the layer.

Windows 〔Ctrl〕-〔Shift〕-〔←〕, 〔Ctrl〕-〔Shift〕-〔→〕, 〔Ctrl〕-〔Shift〕-〔↑〕, 〔Ctrl〕-〔Shift〕-〔↓〕,
  Mac 〔⌘〕-〔Shift〕-〔←〕, 〔⌘〕-〔Shift〕-〔→〕, 〔⌘〕-〔Shift〕-〔↑〕, 〔⌘〕-〔Shift〕-〔↓〕

   Move all objects on the layer by ten pixels

   This shortcut works only when there is no selection on the layer.

Photoshop

Keyboard Shortcuts for Cropping

Windows [Enter] and Crop tool, *Mac* [Return] and Crop tool

Accept the cropping

Windows [Esc] and Crop tool, *Mac* [Esc] and Crop tool

Cancel the cropping

Windows [/], *Mac* [/]

Toggle the crop shield on and off

Working with Tools

This section discusses keyboard shortcuts for displaying and hiding tools, for activating tools, and for working with them.

Keyboard Shortcuts for Displaying and Hiding Tools

Windows [F5], *Mac* [F5]

Toggle the display of the Brushes palette

Windows [F6], *Mac* [F6]

Toggle the display of the Color palette

Windows [F7], *Mac* [F7]

Toggle the display of the Layers palette

Windows [F8], *Mac* [F8]

Toggle the display of the Info palette

Windows [F9], [Alt]-[F9], *Mac* [Option]-[F9]

Toggle the display of the Actions palette

Keyboard Shortcuts for Working with Tools

Windows [M], *Mac* [M]

Activate the Marquee tool

Press Shift-M to toggle between the Rectangular Marquee tool and the Elliptical Marquee tool.

Windows V*, Mac* V

> *Activate the Move tool*

Windows L*, Mac* L

> *Activate the Lasso tool*

Press Shift-L to switch among the Lasso tool, the Polygonal Lasso tool, and the Magnetic Lasso tool.

Windows W*, Mac* W

> *Activate the Magic Wand tool*

Windows C*, Mac* C

> *Activate the Crop tool*

Windows K*, Mac* K

> *Activate the Slice tool*

Press Shift-K to toggle between the Slice tool and the Slice Select tool.

Windows J*, Mac* J

> *Activate the Healing Brush tool*

Press Shift-J to switch among the Healing Brush tool, the Patch tool, and the Color Replacement tool.

Windows B*, Mac* B

> *Activate the Brush tool*

Press Shift-B to toggle between the Brush tool and the Pencil tool.

Windows S*, Mac* S

> *Activate the Clone Stamp tool*

Press Shift-S to toggle between the Clone Stamp tool and the Pattern Stamp tool.

Windows Y*, Mac* Y

> *Activate the History Brush tool*

Press Shift-Y to toggle between the History Brush tool and the Art History Brush tool.

Windows [E], *Mac* [E]

Activate the Eraser tool

Press [Shift]-[E] to switch among the Eraser tool, the Background Eraser tool, and the Magic Eraser tool.

Windows [G], *Mac* [G]

Activate the Gradient tool

Press [Shift]-[G] to toggle between the Gradient tool and the Paint Bucket tool.

Windows [R], *Mac* [R]

Activate the Blur tool

Press [Shift]-[R] to switch among the Blur tool, the Sharpen tool, and the Smudge tool.

Windows [O], *Mac* [O]

Activate the Dodge tool

Press [Shift]-[O] to switch among the Dodge tool, the Burn tool, and the Sponge tool.

Windows [A], *Mac* [A]

Activate the Path Selection tool

Press [Shift]-[A] to toggle between the Path Selection tool and the Direct Selection tool.

Windows [T], *Mac* [T]

Activate the Horizontal Type tool

Press [Shift]-[T] to switch among the Horizontal Type tool, the Vertical Type tool, the Horizontal Type Mask tool, and the Vertical Type Mask tool.

Windows [P], *Mac* [P]

Activate the Pen tool

Press [Shift]-[P] to toggle between the Pen tool and the Freeform Pen tool.

Windows [U], *Mac* [U]

Activate the Rectangle tool

Press [Shift]-[U] to switch among the Rectangle tool, the Rounded Rectangle tool, the Ellipse tool, the Polygon tool, the Line tool, and the Custom Shape tool.

Windows [N], *Mac* [N]

Activate the Notes tool

Press [Shift]-[N] to toggle between the Notes tool and the Audio Annotation tool.

Windows [I], *Mac* [I]

Activate the Eyedropper tool

Press [Shift]-[I] to switch among the Eyedropper tool, the Color Sampler tool, and the Measure tool.

Windows [H], *Mac* [H]

Activate the Hand tool

Windows [Z], *Mac* [Z]

Activate the Zoom tool

Press [Alt] (on Windows) or [Option] (on the Mac) to toggle from the Zoom In tool to the Zoom Out tool.

Making Adjustments, Transforms, Blending, and Painting

This section discusses Photoshop's shortcuts for the following:

- Invoking frequently used commands on the Image | Adjustments menu
- Performing transforms
- Feathering and filling
- Switching among edit and screen modes
- Working with blending modes
- Dodging and burning shadows, midtones, and highlights
- Painting objects

Keyboard Shortcuts for Making Adjustments to Images

Windows [Ctrl]-[L], *Mac* [⌘]-[L]

Display the Levels dialog box

Use the Levels dialog box (the Windows version is shown here) to adjust an image's color balance and tonal range.

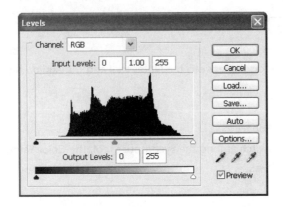

Windows Ctrl -Shift -L , *Mac* ⌘ -Shift -L

Issue an Auto Levels command

Use the Auto Levels command to automatically adjust an image's black point and white point, mapping the lightest pixel in each color channel to level 255 (pure white) and the darkest pixel to level 0 (pure black).

Windows Ctrl -Alt -Shift -L , *Mac* ⌘ -Option -Shift -L

Issue an Auto Contrast command

Use the Auto Contrast command to quickly adjust an image's overall contrast and color mixture.

Windows Ctrl -Shift -B , *Mac* ⌘ -Shift -B

Issue an Auto Color command

Use the Auto Color command to quickly adjust an image's contrast and color.

Windows Ctrl -M , *Mac* ⌘ -M

Display the Curves dialog box

From the Curves dialog box (the Mac version is shown here), you can use the following shortcuts to display the different channels instead of using the Channel drop-down list:

Windows	*Mac*	*RGB Channel*	*CMYK Channel*	*Lightness Channel*
Ctrl -~	⌘ -~	RGB	CMYK	—
Ctrl -1	⌘ -1	Red	Cyan	Lightness
Ctrl -2	⌘ -2	Green	Magenta	a
Ctrl -3	⌘ -3	Blue	Yellow	b
Ctrl -4	⌘ -4	—	Black	—

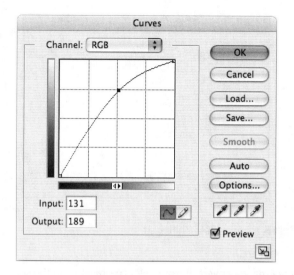

>> **Tip:** *To display the RGB channel or CMYK channel in the Curves dialog box, you can press* Ctrl-` *or* ⌘-` *instead of* Ctrl-~ *or* ⌘-~. *(In other words, you don't need to press* Shift *when using this shortcut with a conventional keyboard layout.)*

Windows Ctrl-B, *Mac* ⌘-B

Display the Color Balance dialog box

Windows Ctrl-U, *Mac* ⌘-U

Display the Hue/Saturation dialog box

From the Hue/Saturation dialog box (the Windows version is shown here), you can use the following shortcuts to change color or hue instead of using the Edit drop-down list:

Windows	**Mac**	**Color**
Ctrl-~	⌘-~	Master
Ctrl-1	⌘-1	Reds
Ctrl-2	⌘-2	Yellows
Ctrl-3	⌘-3	Greens
Ctrl-4	⌘-4	Cyans
Ctrl-5	⌘-5	Blues
Ctrl-6	⌘-6	Magentas

Photoshop

Windows [Ctrl]-[Shift]-[U], *Mac* [⌘]-[Shift]-[U]

Desaturate the image

Desaturating an image converts it from color to grayscale in the same color mode.

Windows [Ctrl]-[I], *Mac* [⌘]-[I]

Invert the colors in the image

Keyboard Shortcuts for Transforms

Photoshop's Free Transform command enables you to apply multiple transformations quickly and easily.

Windows [Ctrl]-[T], *Mac* [⌘]-[T]

Invoke the Free Transform command

After selecting a handle on the bounding box and invoking the Free Transform command, you can use the following keyboard-mouse combinations to transform the object:

Windows	**Mac**	**Effect**
[Shift]-drag	[Shift]-drag	Scale proportionately
[Alt]-drag	[Option]-drag	Distort relative to the center point of the bounding border
[Ctrl]-drag	[⌘]-drag	Distort freely
[Ctrl]-[Shift]-drag	[⌘]-[Shift]-drag	Skew (drag a side handle)
[Ctrl]-[Alt]-[Shift]-drag	[⌘]-[Option]-[Shift]-drag	Apply perspective

When you've finished transforming the object, press [Enter] (on Windows) or [Return] (on the Mac) to commit the transformation. Press [Esc] on either platform to cancel the transformation.

Windows Ctrl - Shift - T, *Mac* ⌘ - Shift - T

Transform again

Windows Ctrl - Alt - T, *Mac* ⌘ - Option - T

Perform a free transform with duplicate data

Windows Ctrl - Alt - Shift - T, *Mac* ⌘ - Option - Shift - T

Transform again with duplicate data

Keyboard Shortcuts for Feathering and Filling

Windows Ctrl - Alt - D, Shift - F6, *Mac* ⌘ - Option - D, Shift - F6

Display the Feather Selection dialog box

Use the Feather Selection dialog box (the Mac version is shown here) to define a feathered edge for the selection.

Windows Shift - F5, Shift - Backspace, *Mac* Shift - F5, Shift - Delete

Display the Fill dialog box

Use the Fill dialog box (the Windows version is shown here) to specify fill contents and blending.

Keyboard Shortcuts for Switching Among Edit and Screen Modes

Windows Q, *Mac* Q

   Toggle between Edit In Standard Mode and Edit In Quick Mask Mode

Windows F, *Mac* F

   Switch among Standard Screen Mode, Full Screen Mode With Menu Bar, and Full Screen Mode

Keyboard Shortcuts for Working with Blending Modes

Windows Alt-Shift-+, Alt-Shift--, *Mac* Option-Shift-+, Option-Shift--

   Cycle through the blending modes

Windows Alt-Shift-N, *Mac* Option-Shift-N

   Normal

Windows Alt-Shift-I, *Mac* Option-Shift-I

   Dissolve

Windows Alt-Shift-Q, *Mac* Option-Shift-Q

   Behind

Windows Alt-Shift-R, *Mac* Option-Shift-R

   Clear

Windows Alt-Shift-K, *Mac* Option-Shift-K

   Darken

Windows Alt-Shift-M, *Mac* Option-Shift-M

   Multiply

Windows Alt-Shift-B, *Mac* Option-Shift-B

   Color Burn

Windows Alt-Shift-A, *Mac* Option-Shift-A

   Linear Burn

Windows [Alt]-[Shift]-[G], *Mac* [Option]-[Shift]-[G]

Lighten

Windows [Alt]-[Shift]-[S], *Mac* [Option]-[Shift]-[S]

Screen

Windows [Alt]-[Shift]-[D], *Mac* [Option]-[Shift]-[D]

Color Dodge

Windows [Alt]-[Shift]-[W], *Mac* [Option]-[Shift]-[W]

Linear Dodge

Windows [Alt]-[Shift]-[O], *Mac* [Option]-[Shift]-[O]

Overlay

Windows [Alt]-[Shift]-[F], *Mac* [Option]-[Shift]-[F]

Soft Light

Windows [Alt]-[Shift]-[H], *Mac* [Option]-[Shift]-[H]

Hard Light

Windows [Alt]-[Shift]-[V], *Mac* [Option]-[Shift]-[V]

Vivid Light

Windows [Alt]-[Shift]-[J], *Mac* [Option]-[Shift]-[J]

Linear Light

Windows [Alt]-[Shift]-[Z], *Mac* [Option]-[Shift]-[Z]

Pin Light

Windows [Alt]-[Shift]-[L], *Mac* [Option]-[Shift]-[L]

Hard Mix

Windows [Alt]-[Shift]-[E], *Mac* [Option]-[Shift]-[E]

Difference

Photoshop

Windows [Alt]-[Shift]-[X], *Mac* [Option]-[Shift]-[X]
Exclusion

Windows [Alt]-[Shift]-[U], *Mac* [Option]-[Shift]-[U]
Hue

Windows [Alt]-[Shift]-[C], *Mac* [Option]-[Shift]-[C]
Color

Windows [Alt]-[Shift]-[Y], *Mac* [Option]-[Shift]-[Y]
Luminosity

Windows [Alt]-[Shift]-[T], *Mac* [Option]-[Shift]-[T]
Saturation

Windows [Alt]-[Shift]-[S] and Sponge tool, *Mac* [Option]-[Shift]-[S] and Sponge tool
Saturate

Windows [Alt]-[Shift]-[D] and Sponge tool, *Mac* [Option]-[Shift]-[D] and Sponge tool
Desaturate

Keyboard Shortcuts for Dodging and Burning Shadows, Midtones, and Highlights

Windows [Alt]-[Shift]-[S] and Dodge tool, *Mac* [Option]-[Shift]-[S] and Dodge tool
Dodge shadows

Windows [Alt]-[Shift]-[M] and Dodge tool, *Mac* [Option]-[Shift]-[M] and Dodge tool
Dodge midtones

Windows [Alt]-[Shift]-[H] and Dodge tool, *Mac* [Option]-[Shift]-[H] and Dodge tool
Dodge highlights

Windows [Alt]-[Shift]-[S] and Burn tool, *Mac* [Option]-[Shift]-[S] and Burn tool
Burn shadows

Windows [Alt]-[Shift]-[M] and Burn tool, *Mac* [Option]-[Shift]-[M] and Burn tool

Burn midtones

Windows [Alt]-[Shift]-[H] and Burn tool, *Mac* [Option]-[Shift]-[H] and Burn tool

Burn highlights

Keyboard Shortcuts for Working with the Painting Tools

Windows [Shift]-[+], *Mac* [Shift]-[+]

Cycle through the blending modes for the painting tools

Windows [/], *Mac* [/]

Lock transparent pixels on or off

Windows [Alt]-[Backspace], *Mac* [Option]-[Delete]

Fill the selection or layer with the foreground color

Windows [Alt]-[Shift]-[Backspace], *Mac* [Option]-[Shift]-[Delete]

Fill only the areas that contain pixels with the foreground color

Windows [Ctrl]-[Backspace], *Mac* [⌘]-[Delete]

Fill the selection or layer with the background color

Windows [Ctrl]-[Shift]-[Backspace], *Mac* [⌘]-[Shift]-[Delete]

Fill only the areas that contain pixels with the background color

Windows [Ctrl]-[Alt]-[Backspace], *Mac* [⌘]-[Option]-[Delete]

Fill from history

Working with Layers

Photoshop includes keyboard shortcuts for performing common operations with layers: creating new layers from scratch, and creating them via copying or cutting a selection; creating and releasing the clipping mask; and arranging layers into the right order.

Photoshop

Keyboard Shortcuts for Creating Layers

Windows [Ctrl]-[Shift]-[N], *Mac* [⌘]-[Shift]-[N]

Display the New Layer dialog box

Use the New Layer dialog box (the Windows version is shown here) to create a new layer in the active image.

Windows [Ctrl]-[J], *Mac* [⌘]-[J]

Create a new layer by copying the current selection

Windows [Ctrl]-[Shift]-[J], *Mac* [⌘]-[Shift]-[J]

Create a new layer by cutting the current selection

Keyboard Shortcuts for Creating and Releasing the Clipping Mask

Windows [Ctrl]-[G], *Mac* [⌘]-[G]

Create a clipping mask

Use a clipping mask to control whether one or more successive layers masks the layers above it or them. To create the mask, select the layer or layers in the Layers palette, and then press this shortcut or choose Layer | Create Clipping Mask.

Windows [Ctrl]-[Shift]-[G], *Mac* [⌘]-[Shift]-[G]

Release the selected clipping mask

Use this shortcut (or choose Layers | Release Clipping Mask) to remove a clipping mask you've applied.

Keyboard Shortcuts for Arranging Layers

Windows [Ctrl]-[]], *Mac* [⌘]-[]]

Bring the selected layer forward

Windows Ctrl-[], *Mac* ⌘-[]

Send the selected layer backward

Windows Ctrl-Shift-[], *Mac* ⌘-Shift-[]

Bring the selected layer to the front

Windows Ctrl-Shift-[], *Mac* ⌘-Shift-[]

Send the selected layer to the back

Keyboard Shortcuts for Merging and Stamping Layers

Windows Ctrl-E, *Mac* ⌘-E

Merge the selected layers

Windows Ctrl-Shift-E, *Mac* ⌘-Shift-E

Merge the visible layers

Windows Ctrl-Alt-E, *Mac* ⌘-Option-E

Stamp the selected layer with the contents of the layer beneath it

When working with linked layers, select one linked layer and press this shortcut to stamp that layer with the contents of the other linked layers.

Windows Ctrl-Alt-Shift-E, *Mac* ⌘-Option-Shift-E

Stamp the selected layer with all visible layers

Use this command as an alternative to the Merge Visible command.

Working with Filters

Photoshop provides keyboard shortcuts for reapplying the last filter, displaying the Extract dialog box, and displaying the Pattern Maker dialog box. (You can create custom shortcuts for further filter operations if you need to perform them often.)

Keyboard Shortcuts for Working with Filters

Windows Ctrl-F, *Mac* ⌘-F

Apply the last filter

Use this shortcut to quickly apply the last filter you used again—for example, to the next image that you need to work with.

Photoshop

Windows ⌷Ctrl⌷-⌷Alt⌷-⌷X⌷, *Mac* ⌷⌘⌷-⌷Option⌷-⌷X⌷

Display the Extract dialog box

Use the Extract dialog box to create a filter to isolate an object in the foreground of an image.

Windows ⌷Ctrl⌷-⌷Alt⌷-⌷Shift⌷-⌷X⌷, *Mac* ⌷⌘⌷-⌷Option⌷-⌷Shift⌷-⌷X⌷

Display the Pattern Maker dialog box

Use the Pattern Maker dialog box to create patterns based on the current selection or on an item copied or cut to the Clipboard.

Working with Text

Photoshop supports not only some standard keyboard shortcuts for selecting characters, words, and lines, but also shortcuts for quickly aligning text, working with fonts, and adjusting kerning, tracking, and leading.

Keyboard Shortcuts for Selecting Text

Windows ⌷Shift⌷-⌷←⌷, *Mac* ⌷Shift⌷-⌷←⌷

Select one character to the left

Windows ⌷Shift⌷-⌷→⌷, *Mac* ⌷Shift⌷-⌷→⌷

Select one character to the right

Windows ⌷Shift⌷-⌷↑⌷, *Mac* ⌷Shift⌷-⌷↑⌷

Select one line up

If the cursor is at the end of the line, this shortcut selects the current line.

Windows ⌷Shift⌷-⌷↓⌷, *Mac* ⌷Shift⌷-⌷↓⌷

Select one line down

Windows ⌷Ctrl⌷-⌷Shift⌷-⌷←⌷, *Mac* ⌷⌘⌷-⌷Shift⌷-⌷←⌷

Select one word to the left

Windows ⌷Ctrl⌷-⌷Shift⌷-⌷→⌷, *Mac* ⌷⌘⌷-⌷Shift⌷-⌷→⌷

Select one word to the right

Windows [Ctrl]-[H], *Mac* [⌘]-[H]

Show or hide the selection on selected text

Keyboard Shortcuts for Aligning Text

Windows [Ctrl]-[Shift]-[L] and Horizontal Type tool,
Mac [⌘]-[Shift]-[L] and Horizontal Type tool

Left-align the text

Windows [Ctrl]-[Shift]-[R] and Horizontal Type tool,
Mac [⌘]-[Shift]-[R] and Horizontal Type tool

Right-align the text

Windows [Ctrl]-[Shift]-[C] and Horizontal Type tool,
Mac [⌘]-[Shift]-[C] and Horizontal Type tool

Center the text

Windows [Ctrl]-[Shift]-[L] and Vertical Type tool,
Mac [⌘]-[Shift]-[L] and Vertical Type tool

Top-align the text

Windows [Ctrl]-[Shift]-[R] and Vertical Type tool,
Mac [⌘]-[Shift]-[R] and Vertical Type tool

Bottom-align the text

Windows [Ctrl]-[Shift]-[C] and Vertical Type tool,
Mac [⌘]-[Shift]-[C] and Vertical Type tool

Center the text vertically

Windows [Ctrl]-[Shift]-[J], *Mac* [⌘]-[Shift]-[J]

Justify the paragraph
Standard justification leaves the last line of the paragraph aligned left.

Windows [Ctrl]-[Shift]-[F], *Mac* [⌘]-[Shift]-[F]

Justify the paragraph, including the last line
Press this shortcut to force justification on the last line of the paragraph, making it justified rather than aligned left.

Photoshop

Keyboard Shortcuts for Working with Fonts

Windows [Ctrl]-[Shift]-[Y], *Mac* [⌘]-[Shift]-[Y]

Restore the default font style

Windows [Ctrl]-[Shift]-[>], *Mac* [⌘]-[Shift]-[>]

Increase the font size by two points

Windows [Ctrl]-[Alt]-[Shift]-[>], *Mac* [⌘]-[Option]-[Shift]-[>]

Increase the font size by ten points

Windows [Ctrl]-[Shift]-[<], *Mac* [⌘]-[Shift]-[<]

Decrease the font size by two points

Windows [Ctrl]-[Alt]-[Shift]-[<], *Mac* [⌘]-[Option]-[Shift]-[<]

Decrease the font size by ten points

Windows [Alt]-[Shift]-[↓], *Mac* [Option]-[Shift]-[↓]

Decrease the baseline shift by two points

Windows [Ctrl]-[Alt]-[Shift]-[↓], *Mac* [⌘]-[Option]-[Shift]-[↓]

Decrease the baseline shift by ten points

Windows [Alt]-[Shift]-[↑], *Mac* [Option]-[Shift]-[↑]

Increase the baseline shift by two points

Windows [Ctrl]-[Alt]-[Shift]-[↑], *Mac* [⌘]-[Option]-[Shift]-[↑]

Increase the baseline shift by ten points

Windows [Ctrl]-[Shift]-[X], *Mac* [⌘]-[Shift]-[X]

Apply 100 percent horizontal scale

Windows [Ctrl]-[Alt]-[Shift]-[X], *Mac* [⌘]-[Option]-[Shift]-[X]

Apply 100 percent vertical scale

Keyboard Shortcuts for Kerning, Tracking, Leading, and Hyphenation

Windows [Ctrl]-[Alt]-[Shift]-[A], *Mac* [⌘]-[Option]-[Shift]-[A]

Apply auto leading

Windows [Alt]-[↓], *Mac* [Option]-[↓]

Increase the leading by two points

Windows [Ctrl]-[Alt]-[↓], *Mac* [⌘]-[Option]-[↓]

Increase the leading by ten points

Windows [Alt]-[↑], *Mac* [Option]-[↑]

Decrease the leading by two points

Windows [Ctrl]-[Alt]-[↑], *Mac* [⌘]-[Option]-[↑]

Decrease the leading by ten points

Windows [Ctrl]-[Shift]-[Q], *Mac* [⌘]-[Ctrl]-[Shift]-[Q]

Apply zero tracking

Windows [Alt]-[←], *Mac* [Option]-[←]

Decrease kerning or tracking by 20/1000 em

Windows [Alt]-[→], *Mac* [Option]-[→]

Increase kerning or tracking by 20/1000 em

Windows [Ctrl]-[Shift]-[Alt]-[H], *Mac* [⌘]-[Ctrl]-[Option]-[Shift]-[H]

Toggle paragraph hyphenation on or off

Windows [Ctrl]-[Alt]-[Shift]-[T], *Mac* [⌘]-[Option]-[Shift]-[T]

Toggle between single composer and every-line composer

Working with Palettes

Photoshop enables you to perform many actions in palettes with keyboard shortcuts or by using one or more modifier keys in combination with a click or another mouse action. This section starts by discussing the keyboard shortcuts that work in most (or all) palettes. It then covers the keyboard shortcuts that work only in specific palettes.

Keyboard Shortcuts for Working with Palettes

Windows ⎡Tab⎤, *Mac* ⎡Tab⎤

Toggle the display of all palettes

Windows ⎡Shift⎤-⎡Tab⎤, *Mac* ⎡Shift⎤-⎡Tab⎤

Toggle the display of all palettes excerpt the Toolbox and the Options bar

Windows ⎡Shift⎤-⎡↑⎤, *Mac* ⎡Shift⎤-⎡↑⎤

Increase units by ten in a shortcut menu

Windows ⎡Shift⎤-⎡↓⎤, *Mac* ⎡Shift⎤-⎡↓⎤

Decrease units by ten in a shortcut menu

Windows ⎡Alt⎤-click the New button, *Mac* ⎡Option⎤-click the New button

Set options

This shortcut doesn't work for the Actions palette, the Styles palette, the Brushes palette, the Tool Presets palette, and the Layer Comps palette.

Windows ⎡Alt⎤-click the Trash button, *Mac* ⎡Option⎤-click the Trash button

Delete the item without confirmation

This shortcut doesn't work in the Brushes palette.

Windows ⎡Ctrl⎤-click, *Mac* ⎡⌘⎤-click

Load the item as a selection

⎡Ctrl⎤-click or ⎡⌘⎤-click a channel, layer, or path thumbnail to load it as a selection.

Windows ⎡Ctrl⎤-⎡Shift⎤-click, *Mac* ⎡⌘⎤-⎡Shift⎤-click

Add the item to the current selection

⎡Ctrl⎤-⎡Shift⎤-click or ⎡⌘⎤-⎡Shift⎤-click a channel, layer, or path thumbnail to add it to the current selection.

Windows Ctrl-Alt-click, *Mac* ⌘-Option-click

Remove the item from the current selection

Ctrl-Alt-click or ⌘-Option-click a channel, layer, or path thumbnail to remove it from the current selection.

Windows Ctrl-Alt-Shift-click, *Mac* ⌘-Option-Shift-click

Make the item intersect with the current selection

Ctrl-Alt-Shift-click or ⌘-Option-Shift-click a channel, layer, or path thumbnail to make it intersect with the current selection.

Keyboard Shortcuts for Working in the Brushes Palette

Windows Alt-click the brush, *Mac* Option-click the brush

Delete the brush

Windows], *Mac*]

Increase the brush size

Windows [, *Mac* [

Decrease the brush size

Windows Shift-], *Mac* Shift-]

Increase the brush hardness by 25 percent

Windows Shift-[, *Mac* Shift-[

Decrease the brush hardness by 25 percent

Windows ,, *Mac* ,

Select the previous brush size

Windows ., *Mac* .

Select the next brush size

Windows Shift-,, *Mac* Shift-,

Select the first brush

Photoshop

Windows Shift-[.], *Mac* Shift-[.]

Select the last brush

Windows CapsLock, *Mac* CapsLock

Display the precise crosshair for the brush

Windows Alt-Shift-P, *Mac* Option-Shift-P

Toggle the Airbrush option

Keyboard Shortcuts for Working in the Color Palette

Windows Alt-click the Color bar, *Mac* Option-click the Color bar

Select the background color

Windows Shift-click the Color bar, *Mac* Shift-click the Color bar

Cycle through the color models

Keyboard Shortcuts for Working in the Layer Comps Palette

Windows Alt-click the Create New Layer Comp button,
Mac Option-click the Create New Layer Comp button

Create a new layer comp without displaying the New Layer Comp dialog box

Keyboard Shortcuts for Working with the Layers Palette

Windows Alt-click the New Layer button,
Mac Option-click the New Layer button

Create a new layer using the New Layer dialog box

Windows Ctrl-click the New Layer button,
Mac ⌘-click the New Layer button

Create a new layer below the target layer

Windows Ctrl-click a layer thumbnail, *Mac* ⌘-click a layer thumbnail

Load the layer transparency as a selection

Windows [Ctrl]-[E], *Mac* [⌘]-[E]

    Merge down

Windows [Ctrl]-[Shift]-[E], *Mac* [⌘]-[Shift]-[E]

    Merge the visible layers

Windows [Ctrl]-[Alt]-[Shift]-[E], *Mac* [⌘]-[Option]-[Shift]-[E]

    Merge a copy of all the visible layers into the target layer

Windows [Alt]-[[], *Mac* [Option]-[[]

    Activate the next layer down

Windows [Alt]-[]], *Mac* [Option]-[]]

    Activate the next layer up

Windows [Alt]-[Shift]-[]], *Mac* [Option]-[Shift]-[]]

    Activate the top layer

Windows [Alt]-[Shift]-[[], *Mac* [Option]-[Shift]-[[]

    Activate the bottom layer

Windows [Ctrl]-[Shift]-[]], *Mac* [⌘]-[Shift]-[]]

    Bring the target layer to the front of the set

Windows [Ctrl]-[Shift]-[[], *Mac* [⌘]-[Shift]-[[]

    Send the target layer to the back of the set

Windows [Alt]-[Shift]-[P], *Mac* [Option]-[Shift]-[P]

    Pass through blending mode for the layer set

Windows [Alt]-click the eye icon, *Mac* [Option]-click the eye icon

    Toggle the display of all currently visible layers other than the active layer

Windows [/], *Mac* [/]

    Toggle lock transparency for the target layer

Photoshop

Working with Dialog Boxes

In Photoshop's dialog boxes, you can use standard keyboard shortcuts, such as pressing [Tab] to cycle forward through the main controls and [Shift]-[Tab] to cycle backward. The major dialog boxes, such as the Extract dialog box, the Liquify dialog box, and the Pattern Maker dialog box, also support further shortcuts that enable you to quickly access the tools and features you need.

Keyboard Shortcuts for the Extract Dialog Box

Windows [B], *Mac* [B]

Activate the Edge Highlighter tool

Windows [G], *Mac* [G]

Activate the Fill tool

Windows [I], *Mac* [I]

Activate the Eyedropper tool

Windows [C], *Mac* [C]

Activate the Cleanup tool

Windows [T], *Mac* [T]

Activate the Edge Touchup tool

Windows [Spacebar], *Mac* [Spacebar]

Temporarily activate the Hand tool

Windows [Alt], *Mac* [Option]

Change the Cancel button to a Reset button

Windows []], *Mac* []]

Increase the brush size

Windows [[], *Mac* [[]

Decrease the brush size

Windows ⟨Ctrl⟩-⟨0⟩, *Mac* ⟨⌘⟩-⟨0⟩

   Make the image fit in the window

Windows ⟨Ctrl⟩-⟨Spacebar⟩, *Mac* ⟨⌘⟩-⟨Spacebar⟩

   Temporarily select the Zoom In tool

Windows ⟨Alt⟩, ⟨Alt⟩-⟨Spacebar⟩, *Mac* ⟨Option⟩-⟨Spacebar⟩

   Temporarily select the Zoom Out tool

Windows ⟨Alt⟩, *Mac* ⟨Option⟩

   Toggle between the Edge Highlighter tool and the Eraser tool

Windows ⟨Ctrl⟩ with the Edge Highlighter tool selected, *Mac* ⟨⌘⟩ with the Edge Highlighter tool selected

   Toggle Smart Highlighting on and off

Windows ⟨Ctrl⟩-⟨Delete⟩, *Mac* ⟨⌘⟩-⟨Delete⟩

   Highlight the entire image

Windows ⟨Alt⟩-⟨Delete⟩, *Mac* ⟨Option⟩-⟨Delete⟩

   Remove the current highlight

Windows ⟨Shift⟩-click with the Fill tool selected, *Mac* ⟨Shift⟩-click with the Fill tool selected

   Fill the foreground area and preview the extraction

Windows ⟨Ctrl⟩-drag, *Mac* ⟨⌘⟩-drag

   Move the Mask when the Edge Touchup tool is active

Windows ⟨Alt⟩-drag, *Mac* ⟨Option⟩-drag

   Add opacity when the Cleanup tool is active

Windows ⟨X⟩, *Mac* ⟨X⟩

   Toggle the Show menu options between Original and Extracted in Preview

Photoshop

Windows Shift-X, *Mac* Shift-X

Enable the Cleanup tool and Edge Touchup tool before preview

Windows F, *Mac* F

Cycle forward through the items in the Display menu

Windows Shift-F, *Mac* Shift-F

Cycle backward through the items in the Display menu

Windows 0 to 9, *Mac* 0 to 9

Set the strength of the Cleanup tool or the Edge Touchup tool

Keyboard Shortcuts for the Liquify Dialog Box

Windows W, *Mac* W

Activate the Forward Warp tool

Windows R, *Mac* R

Activate the Reconstruct tool

Windows C, *Mac* C

Activate the Twirl Clockwise tool

Windows S, *Mac* S

Activate the Pucker tool

Windows B, *Mac* B

Activate the Bloat tool

Windows O, *Mac* O

Activate the Push Left tool

Windows M, *Mac* M

Activate the Mirror tool

Windows T, *Mac* T

Activate the Turbulence tool

Windows F, *Mac* F

Activate the Freeze Mask tool

Windows D, *Mac* D

Activate the Thaw Mask tool

Windows Spacebar, *Mac* Spacebar

Temporarily activate the Hand tool

Windows Alt, *Mac* Option

Change the Cancel button to a Reset button

Windows], *Mac*]

Increase the brush size

Windows [, *Mac* [

Decrease the brush size

Windows Alt, *Mac* Option

Reverse the direction of the tool

This shortcut works for the Bloat tool, the Pucker tool, the Push Left tool, and the Mirror tool.

Keyboard Shortcuts for the Pattern Maker Dialog Box

Windows Spacebar, *Mac* Spacebar

Temporarily activate the Hand tool

Windows Alt, *Mac* Option

Change the Cancel button to a Reset button

Photoshop

Windows Ctrl-O, *Mac* ⌘-O

Make the image fit in the window

Windows Ctrl-Spacebar, *Mac* ⌘-Spacebar

Temporarily select the Zoom In tool

Windows Alt, Alt-Spacebar, *Mac* Option-Spacebar

Temporarily select the Zoom Out tool

Windows Ctrl-D, *Mac* ⌘-D

Delete the current selection

Windows Ctrl-G, *Mac* ⌘-G

Generate the pattern

Windows Alt-Shift-click, *Mac* Option-Shift-click

Make the clicked item intersect with the current selection

Windows X, *Mac* X

Toggle between the original and the generated pattern

Windows Home, *Mac* Home

Select the first tile in the Tile History list

Windows Page Up, ←, *Mac* Page Up, ←

Select the previous tile in the Tile History list

Windows Page Down, →, *Mac* Page Down, →

Select the next tile in the Tile History list

Windows End, *Mac* End

Select the last tile in the Tile History list

Windows [Delete], *Mac* [Delete]

Delete the selected tile from the Tile History list

Windows [←], [→], [↑], [↓], *Mac* [←], [→], [↑], [↓]

Nudge the selection by a small amount in the direction of the arrow

Windows [Shift]-[←], [Shift]-[→], [Shift]-[↑], [Shift]-[↓], *Mac* [Shift]-[←], [Shift]-[→], [Shift]-[↑], [Shift]-[↓]

Nudge the selection by a larger amount in the direction of the arrow

Keyboard Shortcuts for the Filter Gallery

Windows [Alt], *Mac* [Option]

Change the Cancel button to a Reset button

Windows [Ctrl], *Mac* [⌘]

Change the Cancel button to a Default button

Keyboard Shortcuts for the Camera Raw Dialog Box

Windows [Alt]-drag the Exposure slider or Shadows slider, *Mac* [Option]-drag the Exposure slider or Shadows slider

Display the highlights that will be clipped in Preview

Windows [Shift], *Mac* [Shift]

Change the OK button to a Skip button

Use this shortcut to change the OK button to a Skip button so that you can skip converting files when you select multiple files.

Windows [Alt], *Mac* [Option]

Change the OK button to an Update button

Use this shortcut to change the OK button to an Update button so that you can update the settings for selected files without opening them.

Photoshop

Keyboard Shortcuts for the Photomerge Dialog Box

Windows `Alt`, *Mac* `Option`

Change the Cancel button to a Reset button

Windows `←`, `→`, `↑`, `↓`, *Mac* `←`, `→`, `↑`, `↓`

Move the selected image one pixel left, right, up, or down

Windows `Spacebar`, *Mac* `Spacebar`

Switch to the Hand tool

Windows `A`, *Mac* `A`

Activate the Select Image tool

Windows `R`, *Mac* `R`

Activate the Rotate Image tool

Windows `V`, *Mac* `V`

Activate the Set Vanishing Point tool

Windows `Z`, *Mac* `Z`

Activate the Zoom tool

Windows `H`, *Mac* `H`

Activate the Hand tool

Customizing Keyboard Shortcuts

As you've seen so far in this chapter, Photoshop offers a huge number of keyboard shortcuts—but still, many tools, application commands, and palette commands don't have keyboard shortcuts. Photoshop also enables you to customize its default keyboard shortcuts and create keyboard shortcuts of your own for other commands and tools. You can even define multiple sets of keyboard shortcuts so that you can switch from one to another.

To customize keyboard shortcuts, follow these steps:

1. Press [Ctrl]-[Alt]-[Shift]-[K] (in Windows) or [⌘]-[Option]-[Shift]-[K] (on the Mac) or choose Edit | Keyboard Shortcuts to display the Keyboard Shortcuts dialog box. Figure 2-1 shows the Mac version of the Keyboard Shortcuts dialog box with customization under way.

2. In the Set drop-down list, choose which set of keyboard shortcuts to work with:

- Photoshop starts you off with a set called Photoshop Defaults that contains its default keyboard shortcuts.

- To create a new set of shortcuts, click the New Set button. Photoshop displays the Save dialog box and suggests a default name that consists of the name of the current set of keyboard shortcuts and the word

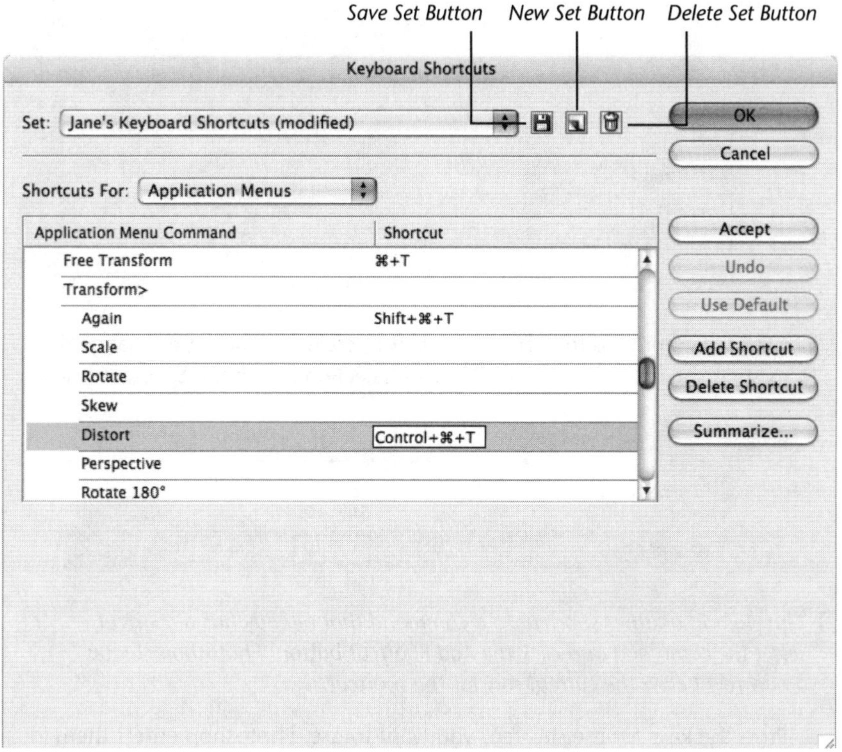

Figure 2-1 *Customize Photoshop's default keyboard shortcuts or create new shortcuts of your own in the Keyboard Shortcuts dialog box.*

Copy—for example, Photoshop Defaults Copy. Change the name and click the Save button. Photoshop selects the new set in the Set drop-down list.

3. In the Shortcuts For drop-down list, select the type of shortcuts you want to work with: Application Menus, Palette Menus, or Tools. Photoshop displays the appropriate categories in the main list box. For example, if you select the Application Menus item, Photoshop displays the application menus as categories.

4. Expand the category of commands you want to work with. For example, to work with a command on the Layer menu, expand the Layer menu category so that you can see its commands:

Application Menu Command	Shortcut
► Edit	
► Image	
▼ Layer	
New>	
Layer...	Shift+⌘+N
Background	
Layer Set...	
Layer Set From Linked...	
Layer via Copy	⌘+J

5. Click the command for which you want to create a shortcut or change the existing shortcut. Photoshop displays a selection box in the Shortcut column:

▼ Layer	
New>	
Layer...	Shift+⌘+N
Background	[ ]

» *Tip: To add another shortcut to a command that already has a shortcut, select the command and click the Add Shortcut button. Photoshop creates a new row below the current row for the shortcut.*

6. Press the keys for the shortcut you want to use. Photoshop enters them in the text box. Click the Accept button to apply the shortcut.

7. If the new shortcut will conflict with an existing shortcut, Photoshop displays a warning, as shown here. Click the Undo Changes button to undo the shortcut, or click the Accept And Go To Conflict button to go to the conflicting existing shortcut so that you can change it.

▼ Layer		Use Default
New>		Add Shortcut
Layer...	Shift+⌘+N	Delete Shortcut
Background	Shift+⌘+X	
Layer Set...		Summarize...
Layer Set From Linked...		
Layer via Copy	⌘+J	

⚠ Shift+⌘+X is already in use and will be removed from Filter > Liquify if accepted.

(Accept and Go To Conflict)   (Undo Changes)

8. To delete a shortcut, select its row and click the Delete Shortcut button.

9. To restore a command to its default shortcut, select it and click the Use Default button.

10. Click the OK button to close the Keyboard Shortcuts dialog box.

To delete a set of shortcuts, select it in the Set drop-down list and click the Delete Set button. In the confirmation dialog box, click the Yes button:

> **Adobe Photoshop**
>
> Are you sure you want to send Jane's Keyboard Shortcuts to the trash?
>
> (No)   (**Yes**)

Automating Tasks in Photoshop

As you've seen so far in this chapter, you can get a lot done in Photoshop by using keyboard shortcuts. But if you use Photoshop extensively, you may want to drive your efficiency to a new level by taking advantage of the following features that Photoshop offers for automating your work:

- **Actions**   Actions are roughly equivalent to macros in many other applications and can provide great power and flexibility. You can't record *every* Photoshop command in an action, but you can record many of them. You can also insert stops in your actions to allow you to perform operations that can't be automated—for example, an edit that needs to be customized to the image in question.

- **Droplets**   After creating an action, you can create a *droplet* from it to give you an easy way of performing the action. A droplet is a miniature application that runs the action. You can save a droplet on your desktop so that it's easily available.

- **Batch processing**   You can use Photoshop's Batch command (File | Automate | Batch) to perform an action or set of actions on one or more folders or files.

- **External automation**   You can use Windows' Automation feature (formerly called Object Linking and Embedding, or OLE) or Mac OS's AppleScript programming language to automate procedures in Photoshop from another application. For example, on the Mac, you might write an AppleScript that you could invoke from Apple's iPhoto application to make Photoshop perform a series of actions on the specified image or images. On Windows, you might use Automation from another application to make Photoshop perform batch-processing of images.

Illustrator Keyboard Shortcuts

Like Photoshop, Illustrator absolutely requires a mouse or drawing pad—but you can get a lot done with the keyboard if you know which keys to press. This chapter shows you how, starting with keyboard shortcuts for basic file operations (such as creating, saving, and printing files) and basic editing operations. The chapter then moves on to changing the view and zoom, displaying and hiding windows, and working with objects. At the end of the chapter, you'll learn about customizing keyboard shortcuts in Illustrator and about automating tasks you need to perform frequently.

Creating, Opening, Saving, Closing, and Printing Files

Your work in Illustrator is almost certain to include opening the files you need to work with (or creating new files from scratch), saving files, closing them, and printing them.

Keyboard Shortcuts for Creating New Files and Opening Existing Files

Windows Ctrl-N, *Mac* ⌘-N

Display the New Document dialog box

In the New Document dialog box (the Mac version is shown in Figure 3-1), specify the name for the document, its size (and units of measurement) and orientation, and its color mode (CMYK Color or RGB Color), and then click the OK button to create it.

Windows Ctrl-Shift-N, *Mac* ⌘-Shift-N

Display the New From Template dialog box

In the New From Template dialog box, select the template on which you want to base the new document, and then click the New button (in Windows) or the New From Template button (on the Mac).

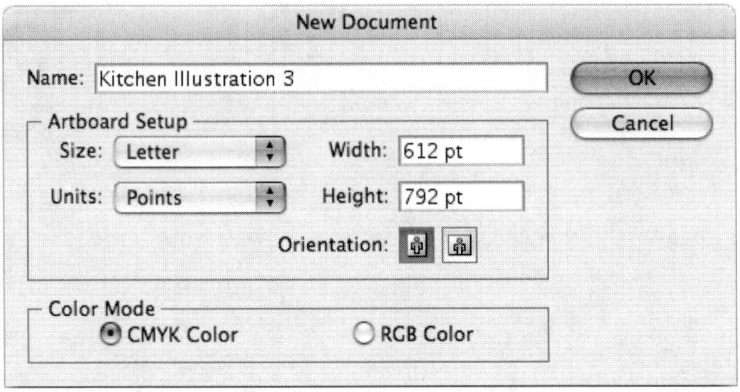

Figure 3-1 *Use the New Document dialog box to set up the new document you're creating.*

Windows [Ctrl]-[O], *Mac* [⌘]-[O]

Display the Open dialog box

Keyboard Shortcuts for Saving and Closing Files

Windows [Ctrl]-[W], [Ctrl]-[F4], *Mac* [⌘]-[W]

Close the active file

If the file contains unsaved changes, Illustrator prompts you to save them.

Windows [Ctrl]-[S], *Mac* [⌘]-[S]

Save the active file

If the active file hasn't been saved before, Illustrator displays the Save As dialog box so that you can specify the folder and the filename under which to save it. Thereafter, if the file contains unsaved changes, Illustrator saves them under the current filename. If the active file doesn't contain any unsaved changes, the Save command is unavailable, and this keyboard shortcut has no effect.

Windows [Ctrl]-[Shift]-[S], *Mac* [⌘]-[Shift]-[S]

Display the Save As dialog box

As discussed in the previous item, Illustrator displays the Save As dialog box when you save a file for the first time. You can also use the Save As dialog box to save a file under a new name, in a different folder, in a different format, or a combination of the three.

Windows Ctrl-Alt-S, *Mac* ⌘-Option-S

Display the Save A Copy dialog box

Use the Save A Copy dialog box to save an identical copy of the active file but to leave the original file active. (By contrast, using a Save As command leaves the new file active.) Saving a copy is great for saving intermediate stages of your work without interrupting its flow.

Windows Ctrl-Alt-Shift-S, *Mac* ⌘-Option-Shift-S

Display the Save For Web dialog box

The Save For Web dialog box offers options for quickly saving the active file in a format optimized for the Web.

Windows Ctrl-Q, Alt-F4, *Mac* ⌘-Q

Quit Illustrator

Keyboard Shortcuts for Changing Document Setup and Printing

Windows Ctrl-Alt-P, *Mac* ⌘-Option-P

Display the Document Setup dialog box

Windows Ctrl-P, *Mac* ⌘-P

Display the Print dialog box

Performing Basic Editing Operations

Illustrator enables you to undo changes you've made, redo changes you've undone, and revert to the last saved version of a file if you've messed up the open version too badly.

Illustrator not only supports extra keyboard shortcuts for Cut, Copy, and Paste operations but also offers keyboard shortcuts for pasting in front and pasting in back. You can also start a spelling check, invoke help, and start configuring Illustrator from the keyboard.

Keyboard Shortcuts for Undo, Redo, and Revert

Windows Ctrl-Z, *Mac* ⌘-Z

Undo the last action

Illustrator lets you undo and redo multiple actions.

Illustrator

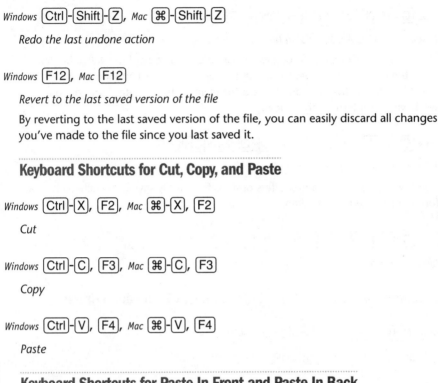

Windows Ctrl-Shift-Z, *Mac* ⌘-Shift-Z

Redo the last undone action

Windows F12, *Mac* F12

Revert to the last saved version of the file

By reverting to the last saved version of the file, you can easily discard all changes you've made to the file since you last saved it.

Keyboard Shortcuts for Cut, Copy, and Paste

Windows Ctrl-X, F2, *Mac* ⌘-X, F2

Cut

Windows Ctrl-C, F3, *Mac* ⌘-C, F3

Copy

Windows Ctrl-V, F4, *Mac* ⌘-V, F4

Paste

Keyboard Shortcuts for Paste In Front and Paste In Back

Windows Ctrl-F, *Mac* ⌘-F

Paste In Front

Press this shortcut to paste an item from the Clipboard in front of the current selection. If there's no selection, Illustrator places the pasted object on the top of the stack.

Windows Ctrl-B, *Mac* ⌘-B

Paste In Back

Press this shortcut to paste an item from the Clipboard behind the current selection. If there's no selection, Illustrator places the pasted object at the back of the stack.

Keyboard Shortcuts for Checking Spelling

Windows Ctrl-I, *Mac* ⌘-I

Displays the Check Spelling dialog box

Keyboard Shortcuts for Getting Help

Windows [F1], *Mac* [F1]

Launch or activate Illustrator Help

Keyboard Shortcuts for Configuring Illustrator

Windows [Ctrl]-[K], *Mac* [⌘]-[K]

Display the General sheet of the Preferences dialog box

Use the Previous button and Next button or the drop-down list in the Preferences dialog box to display other preference sheets.

Windows [Ctrl]-[Shift]-[K], *Mac* [⌘]-[Shift]-[K]

Display the Color Settings dialog box

Windows [Ctrl]-[Alt]-[Shift]-[K], *Mac* [⌘]-[Option]-[Shift]-[K]

Display the Keyboard Shortcuts dialog box

See "Customizing Keyboard Shortcuts," at the end of this chapter, for a discussion of how to customize keyboard shortcuts.

Changing the View and Zoom

To see the objects you want to work with, you'll often need to change the screen mode and the view, zoom the view, and display and hide objects and windows on screen. Illustrator offers keyboard shortcuts for the most common of these operations.

Keyboard Shortcuts for Changing the Screen Mode and View

Windows [F], *Mac* [F]

Toggle the screen mode

Press this shortcut to toggle among Standard mode, Full Screen mode, and Full Screen mode with the menu bar.

Windows [Ctrl]-[Y], *Mac* [⌘]-[Y]

Toggle between Preview and the Outline

Illustrator

Windows Ctrl-Alt-Shift-Y, *Mac* ⌘-Option-Shift-Y

Toggle Overprint Preview on and off

Windows Ctrl-Alt-Y, *Mac* ⌘-Option-Y

Toggle Pixel Preview on and off

Keyboard Shortcuts for Zooming the View

Windows Ctrl-+, *Mac* ⌘-+

Zoom in

Windows Ctrl--, *Mac* ⌘--

Zoom out

Windows Ctrl-0, *Mac* ⌘-0

Zoom the view so that the entire illustration fits in the window

Windows Ctrl-1, *Mac* ⌘-1

Zoom to the illustration's actual size

Windows Ctrl-Spacebar, *Mac* ⌘-Spacebar

Temporarily switch to the Zoom tool in magnify mode

Hold down this shortcut and click with the mouse to magnify the view.

Windows Ctrl-Alt-Spacebar, *Mac* ⌘-Option-Spacebar

Temporarily switch to the Zoom tool in reduce mode

Hold down this shortcut and click with the mouse to reduce the view.

Windows Spacebar, *Mac* Spacebar

Move the Zoom marquee

Press Spacebar to move the Zoom marquee while you're dragging with the zoom tool.

Keyboard Shortcuts for Displaying and Hiding View Items

Windows Ctrl-Alt-Shift-3, *Mac* ⌘-Option-Shift-3

Hide all unselected artwork

Press this shortcut to hide all objects except the selected object.

Windows [Ctrl]-[Alt]-[3], *Mac* [⌘]-[Option]-[3]

> *Display all hidden artwork*
> Press this shortcut to redisplay all hidden objects.

Windows [Ctrl]-[H], *Mac* [⌘]-[H]

> *Hide edges*

Windows [Ctrl]-[Shift]-[W], *Mac* [⌘]-[Shift]-[W]

> *Hide template*

Windows [Ctrl]-[R], *Mac* [⌘]-[R]

> *Toggle the display of the rulers*

Windows [Ctrl]-[Shift]-[B], *Mac* [⌘]-[Shift]-[B]

> *Toggle the display of the bounding box*

Windows [Ctrl]-[Shift]-[D], *Mac* [⌘]-[Shift]-[D]

> *Toggle the display of the transparency grid*

Windows [Ctrl]-[Shift]-[Y], *Mac* [⌘]-[Shift]-[Y]

> *Toggle the display of text threads*

Windows [Ctrl]-["], *Mac* [⌘]-["]

> *Toggle the display of the grid*

Windows [Ctrl]-[Shift]-["], *Mac* [⌘]-[Shift]-["]

> *Toggle the Snap To Pixel feature on and off*

Windows [Ctrl]-[Alt]-["], *Mac* [⌘]-[Option]-["]

> *Toggle the Snap To Point feature on and off*

Keyboard Shortcuts for Working with Guides

Windows [Ctrl]-[U], *Mac* [⌘]-[U]

> *Toggle Smart Guides on and off*

Illustrator

Windows Ctrl-;, *Mac* ⌘-;

> *Toggle the display of guides*

Windows Ctrl-Alt-;, *Mac* ⌘-Option-;

> *Toggle locking on guides*

Windows Ctrl-5, *Mac* ⌘-5

> *Make guides*

Windows Ctrl-Alt-5, *Mac* ⌘-Option-5

> *Release guides*

Windows Alt-drag, *Mac* Option-drag

> *Convert a guide between horizontal and vertical*
>
> Alt-drag or Option-drag the guide you want to convert.

Windows Ctrl-Shift-double-click, *Mac* ⌘-Shift-double-click

> *Release the guide*
>
> Press this shortcut and double-click the guide you want to release.

Keyboard Shortcuts for Displaying and Hiding Windows and Palettes

Windows Alt--, then N, *Mac* ⌘-M

> *Minimize the active window*

Windows Shift-F7, *Mac* Shift-F7

> *Toggle the display of the Align palette*

Windows Shift-F6, *Mac* Shift-F6

> *Toggle the display of the Appearance palette*

Windows F11, *Mac* F11

> *Toggle the display of the Attributes palette*

Windows Shift-F11, *Mac* Shift-F11

> *Toggle the display of the Symbols palette*

>> **Note:** *On Mac OS X version 10.3 (Panther), the* F11 *keyboard shortcut is assigned to the Exposé feature by default. The* Shift-F11 *shortcut slows down the effect of the Exposé animation. So you can't use either of these keyboard shortcuts in Illustrator unless you reassign the Exposé keyboard shortcut in System Preferences.*

Windows F5 , *Mac* F5

    Toggle the display of the Brushes palette

Windows F6 , *Mac* F5

    Toggle the display of the Color palette

Windows F9 , *Mac* F9

    Toggle the display of the Gradient palette

Windows Shift-F5 , *Mac* Shift-F5

    Toggle the display of the Graphic Styles palette

Windows F8 , *Mac* F8

    Toggle the display of the Info palette

Windows F7 , *Mac* F7

    Toggle the display of the Layers palette

Windows Shift-F9 , *Mac* Shift-F9

    Toggle the display of the Pathfinder palette

Windows F10 , *Mac* F10

    Toggle the display of the Stroke palette

Windows Shift-F8 , *Mac* Shift-F8

    Toggle the display of the Transform palette

Windows Shift-F10 , *Mac* Shift-F10

    Toggle the display of the Transparency palette

Illustrator

Working with Objects

Illustrator offers keyboard shortcuts for selecting objects; changing their stacking order; transforming them; and grouping, locking, and hiding them.

Keyboard Shortcuts for Selecting Objects

Windows [Ctrl]-[A], *Mac* [⌘]-[A]

Select all objects

Windows [Ctrl]-[Shift]-[A], *Mac* [⌘]-[Shift]-[A]

Deselect the selection

Windows [Ctrl]-[6], *Mac* [⌘]-[6]

Reselect the selection you've just deselected

Windows [Ctrl]-[Alt]-[]], *Mac* [⌘]-[Option]-[]]

Select the next object above the current object

Windows [Ctrl]-[Alt]-[[], *Mac* [⌘]-[Option]-[[]

Select the next object below the current object

Windows [Ctrl], *Mac* [⌘]

Select the last-used of the selection tools

Windows [Ctrl]-[Tab], *Mac* [⌘]-[Tab]

Toggle between the Selection tool and the Direct Selection tool or the Group Selection tool

When you press this shortcut from the Selection tool, Illustrator switches to whichever tool was last used—the Direct Selection tool or the Group Selection tool. Press this shortcut again to switch back to the Selection tool.

Windows [Shift]-click, *Mac* [Shift]-click

Add the clicked object to, or subtract it from, the current selection

This shortcut works with the Selection tool, the Direct Selection tool, the Group Selection tool, and the Magic Wand tool.

Windows [Shift]-drag, *Mac* [Shift]-drag

Add to the selection with the Lasso tool

Windows [Alt]-drag, *Mac* [Option]-drag

Subtract from the selection with the Lasso tool

Keyboard Shortcuts for Moving Objects

Windows [←], [→], [↑], [↓], *Mac* [←], [→], [↑], [↓]

Move the selection by one increment

When you press an arrow key, Illustrator moves the selection by the increment defined in the Keyboard Increment text box on the General sheet of the Preferences dialog box.

Windows [Shift]-[←], [Shift]-[→], [Shift]-[↑], [Shift]-[↓],
Mac [Shift]-[←], [Shift]-[→], [Shift]-[↑], [Shift]-[↓]

Move the selection by ten increments

Illustrator moves the selection by ten of the increments defined in the Keyboard Increment text box on the General sheet of the Properties dialog box.

Windows [Shift], *Mac* [Shift]

Constrain the movement to a 45-degree angle

This shortcut doesn't work with the Reflect tool.

Keyboard Shortcuts for Changing the Stacking Order of Objects

Windows [Ctrl]-[]], *Mac* [⌘]-[]]

Bring the object forward by one object in the stack

Windows [Ctrl]-[Shift]-[]], *Mac* [⌘]-[Shift]-[]]

Bring the object to the front of the stack

Windows [Ctrl]-[[], *Mac* [⌘]-[[]

Send the object backward by one object in the stack

Windows [Ctrl]-[Shift]-[[], *Mac* [⌘]-[Shift]-[[]

Send the object to the back of the stack

Illustrator

Keyboard Shortcuts for Transforming Objects

Windows [Alt]-click, *Mac* [Option]-click

Set the origin point and display the appropriate dialog box

This shortcut works with the Rotate tool, the Scale tool, the Reflect tool, and the Shear tool. For example, with the Rotate tool selected, [Alt]-click to set the origin point and display the Rotate dialog box.

Windows [Alt]-drag, *Mac* [Option]-drag

Duplicate the selection and transform it

This shortcut works with the Selection tool, the Scale tool, the Reflect tool, and the Shear tool.

Windows [~]-drag, *Mac* [~]-drag

Transform the pattern independent of the object

This shortcut works with the Selection tool, the Scale tool, the Reflect tool, and the Shear tool.

Windows [Ctrl]-[D], *Mac* [⌘]-[D]

Transform again

Press this shortcut to repeat the previous transformation.

Windows [Ctrl]-[Shift]-[M], *Mac* [⌘]-[Shift]-[M]

Display the Move dialog box

In the Move dialog box (the Mac version is shown here), specify how to move the object, and then press [Enter] or [Return].

>> Tip: *After selecting an object, you can also display the Move dialog box by double-clicking the Selection tool, the Direct Selection tool, or the Group Selection tool.*

Windows Ctrl-Alt-Shift-D, *Mac* ⌘-Option-Shift-D

Display the Transform Each dialog box

Use the Transform Each dialog box (the Windows version is shown here) to move multiple objects by the same amount. You can also use the Random option to move the objects randomly up to the distances you specify in the Horizontal text box and Vertical text box in the Move group box.

Keyboard Shortcuts for Grouping and Ungrouping Objects

Windows Ctrl-G, *Mac* ⌘-G

Group the selected objects together

By grouping two or more objects together, you can treat them as a single unit— for example, so that you can move them and format them as if they were a single object.

Windows Ctrl-Shift-G, *Mac* ⌘-Shift-G

Ungroup the selected group of objects

Keyboard Shortcuts for Locking and Unlocking Objects

Windows Ctrl-2, *Mac* ⌘-2

Lock the selected object or objects

Lock an object when you want to make sure you don't select it or edit it.

Windows Ctrl-Alt-2, *Mac* ⌘-Option-2

Unlock all objects

Unlock locked objects when you need to work with them again.

Windows Ctrl-Alt-Shift-2, *Mac* ⌘-Option-Shift-2

Lock all deselected artwork

Keyboard Shortcuts for Hiding and Showing Objects

Windows Ctrl-3, *Mac* ⌘-3

Hide the selection

Hide a selection when you want to prevent yourself from selecting it or modifying it or when you simply want to remove it from view so that you can work with objects that it overlaps.

Windows Ctrl-Alt-3, *Mac* ⌘-Option-3

Show all hidden items

Press this shortcut to display hidden items so that you can see them and work with them again.

Keyboard Shortcuts for Joining and Averaging Paths

Windows Ctrl-J, *Mac* ⌘-J

Join the endpoints of the selected open path

Windows Ctrl-Alt-J, *Mac* ⌘-Option-J

Average two or more anchor points

Use the Average command to move selected anchor points to a new position derived from the average of their current positions. The points can be on different paths or the same path.

Keyboard Shortcuts for Making and Releasing Compound Paths

Windows Ctrl-8, *Mac* ⌘-8

Make a compound path from the selected paths

Windows Ctrl-Alt-8, *Mac* ⌘-Option-8

Release the selected compound path

Keyboard Shortcuts for Blending Objects

Windows ⟨Ctrl⟩-⟨Alt⟩-⟨B⟩, *Mac* ⟨⌘⟩-⟨Option⟩-⟨B⟩

Issue a Make Blend command

Press this shortcut to have Illustrator create intermediate objects between the objects you've selected.

Windows ⟨Ctrl⟩-⟨Alt⟩-⟨Shift⟩-⟨B⟩, *Mac* ⟨⌘⟩-⟨Option⟩-⟨Shift⟩-⟨B⟩

Release the blended objects

Keyboard Shortcuts for Envelope Distort

Windows ⟨Ctrl⟩-⟨Alt⟩-⟨Shift⟩-⟨W⟩, *Mac* ⟨⌘⟩-⟨Option⟩-⟨Shift⟩-⟨W⟩

Display the Warp Options dialog box

In the Warp Options dialog box (the Mac version is shown here), choose the warp style and other options, and then press ⟨Enter⟩ (on Windows) or ⟨Return⟩ (on the Mac).

Windows ⟨Ctrl⟩-⟨Alt⟩-⟨M⟩, *Mac* ⟨⌘⟩-⟨Option⟩-⟨M⟩

Display the Envelope Mesh dialog box

In the Envelope Mesh dialog box (the Windows version is shown here), specify the number of rows and columns for the mesh, and then press ⟨Enter⟩ or ⟨Return⟩.

Windows Ctrl - Alt - C , *Mac* ⌘ - Option - C
Make an envelope with the top object

Windows Ctrl - Shift - V , *Mac* ⌘ - Shift - V
Edit the contents of the selected envelope

Keyboard Shortcuts for Making and Releasing Clipping Masks

Windows Ctrl - 7 , *Mac* ⌘ - 7
Make a clipping mask

Windows Ctrl - Alt - 7 , *Mac* ⌘ - Option - 7
Release the selected clipping mask

Keyboard Shortcuts for Painting Objects

Windows X , *Mac* X
Toggle between fill and stroke

Windows D , *Mac* D
Set the fill and stroke to the default setting

Windows Shift - X , *Mac* Shift - X
Swap the fill and the stroke

Windows . , *Mac* .
Select Gradient Fill mode

Windows , , *Mac* ,
Select Color Fill or Stroke mode

Windows / , *Mac* /
Select No Stroke or No Fill mode

Windows Ctrl - / , *Mac* ⌘ - /
Add a new fill

Windows [Ctrl]-[Alt]-[/], *Mac* [⌘]-[Option]-[/]

Add a new stroke

Windows [Alt], *Mac* [Option]

Toggle between the Paint Bucket tool and the Eyedropper tool

Press this shortcut when the Paint Bucket tool is selected to change temporarily to the Eyedropper tool, and vice versa.

Windows [Shift]-click with Eyedropper tool,
Mac [Shift]-click with Eyedropper tool

Sample the color

Use this shortcut to sample the color from a picture or an intermediate color from a gradient.

Windows [Alt]-[Shift]-click with Eyedropper tool,
Mac [Option]-[Shift]-click with Eyedropper tool

Sample the style and append the appearance of the currently selected item

Windows [Ctrl]-click the Gradient button,
Mac [⌘]-click the Gradient button

Restore the gradient to black and white

Selecting Tools

When you're working, you'll often find that the quickest way to select a tool is by pressing its keyboard shortcut. Illustrator provides single-key shortcuts for most tools.

Keyboard Shortcuts for Selecting Tools

Windows [V], *Mac* [V]

Select the Selection tool

Windows [A], *Mac* [A]

Select the Direct Selection tool

Windows [Y], *Mac* [Y]

Select the Magic Wand tool

Illustrator

Windows Q , *Mac* Q

   Select the Lasso tool

Windows P , *Mac* P

   Select the Pen tool

Windows + , *Mac* +

   Select the Add Anchor Point tool

Windows - , *Mac* -

   Select the Delete Anchor Point tool

Windows Shift - C , *Mac* Shift - C

   Select the Convert Anchor Point tool

Windows T , *Mac* T

   Select the Type tool

Windows \ , *Mac* \

   Select the Line Segment tool

Windows M , *Mac* M

   Select the Rectangle tool

Windows L , *Mac* L

   Select the Ellipse tool

Windows B , *Mac* B

   Select the Paintbrush tool

Windows N , *Mac* N

   Select the Pencil tool

Windows R , *Mac* R

   Select the Rotate tool

Windows ☐O☐, *Mac* ☐O☐

    Select the Reflect tool

Windows ☐S☐, *Mac* ☐S☐

    Select the Scale tool

Windows ☐Shift☐-☐R☐, *Mac* ☐Shift☐-☐R☐

    Select the Warp tool

Windows ☐E☐, *Mac* ☐E☐

    Select the Free Transform tool

Windows ☐Shift☐-☐S☐, *Mac* ☐Shift☐-☐S☐

    Select the Symbol Sprayer tool

Windows ☐J☐, *Mac* ☐J☐

    Select the Column Graph tool

Windows ☐U☐, *Mac* ☐U☐

    Select the Mesh tool

Windows ☐G☐, *Mac* ☐G☐

    Select the Gradient tool

Windows ☐I☐, *Mac* ☐I☐

    Select the Eyedropper tool

Windows ☐K☐, *Mac* ☐K☐

    Select the Paint Bucket tool

Windows ☐W☐, *Mac* ☐W☐

    Select the Blend tool

Windows ☐Shift☐-☐K☐, *Mac* ☐Shift☐-☐K☐

    Select the Slice tool

Illustrator

Windows C, *Mac* C

Select the Scissors tool

Windows H, *Mac* H

Select the Hand tool

Windows Spacebar, *Mac* Spacebar

Temporarily switch to the Hand tool

This shortcut works when Illustrator isn't in text-edit mode.

Windows Z, *Mac* Z

Select the Zoom tool

Working with Text

Beyond the mostly standard keyboard shortcuts for navigating through text and selecting it, Illustrator offers keyboard shortcuts for setting leading, kerning, and alignment.

Keyboard Shortcuts for Navigating Through Text

Windows ←, *Mac* ←

Move to the left by one character

Windows →, *Mac* →

Move to the right by one character

Windows ↑, *Mac* ↑

Move up by one line

Windows ↓, *Mac* ↓

Move down by one line

Windows Ctrl-←, *Mac* ⌘-←

Move to the left by one word

Windows [Ctrl]-[→], *Mac* [⌘]-[→]

Move to the right by one word

Windows [Ctrl]-[↑], *Mac* [⌘]-[↑]

Move up by one paragraph

Windows [Ctrl]-[↓], *Mac* [⌘]-[↓]

Move down by one paragraph

Keyboard Shortcuts for Selecting Text

Windows [Shift]-[←], *Mac* [Shift]-[←]

Select one character to the left

>> **Note:** *These shortcuts work both for extending an existing selection (or creating a new selection) and for reducing an existing selection. For example, you can press* [Shift]-[←] *to decrease an existing selection by one character.*

Windows [Shift]-[→], *Mac* [Shift]-[→]

Select one character to the right

Windows [Ctrl]-[Shift]-[←], *Mac* [⌘]-[Shift]-[←]

Select one word to the left

Windows [Ctrl]-[Shift]-[→], *Mac* [⌘]-[Shift]-[→]

Select one word to the right

Windows [Ctrl]-[Shift]-[↑], *Mac* [⌘]-[Shift]-[↑]

Select one paragraph upward

Windows [Ctrl]-[Shift]-[↓], *Mac* [⌘]-[Shift]-[↓]

Select one paragraph downward

Keyboard Shortcuts for Working with Type

Windows [Shift]-[Enter], *Mac* [Shift]-[Return]

Insert a soft return

Illustrator

Windows [Ctrl]-[Shift]-[X], *Mac* [⌘]-[Shift]-[X]

Reset the horizontal scale to 100 percent

Windows [Ctrl]-[Shift]-[>], *Mac* [⌘]-[Shift]-[>]

Increase the point size

This shortcut and the next change the point size by the increment specified in the Size/Leading text box on the Type & Auto Tracing sheet of the Preferences dialog box.

Windows [Ctrl]-[Shift]-[<], *Mac* [⌘]-[Shift]-[<]

Decrease the point size

Windows [Shift], *Mac* [Shift]

Switch among the Type tools

Press [Shift] to switch temporarily between the Type tool and the Vertical Type tool, the Area Type tool and the Vertical Area Type tool, and the Path Type tool and the Vertical Path Type tool.

Windows [Alt]-click the Type tool, *Mac* [Option]-click the Type tool

Switch between the Area Type tool and the Type tool, the Path Type tool and the Area Type tool, and the Vertical Path Type tool and the Vertical Area Type tool.

Windows [Ctrl]-[Alt]-[I], *Mac* [⌘]-[Option]-[I]

Toggle the display of hidden characters

Windows [Ctrl]-[Shift]-[O], *Mac* [⌘]-[Shift]-[O]

Create outlines

Press this shortcut to convert the selected type into outlines that you can manipulate as graphic objects.

Keyboard Shortcuts for Setting Leading

Windows [Alt]-[↑], *Mac* [Option]-[↑]

Decrease the leading

This shortcut and the next change the leading by the increment specified in the Size/Leading text box on the Type & Auto Tracing sheet of the Preferences dialog box.

Windows [Alt]-[↓], *Mac* [Option]-[↓]

Increase the leading

Windows [Alt]-[Shift]-[↑], *Mac* [Option]-[Shift]-[↑]

Increase the baseline shift

This shortcut and the next change the baseline shift by the increment specified in the Baseline Shift text box on the Type & Auto Tracing sheet of the Preferences dialog box.

Windows [Alt]-[Shift]-[↓], *Mac* [Option]-[Shift]-[↓]

Decrease the baseline shift

Keyboard Shortcuts for Kerning

Windows [Ctrl]-[Alt]-[Q], *Mac* [⌘]-[Option]-[Q]

Reset the tracking and kerning to 0 (zero)

Windows [Ctrl]-[Alt]-[K], *Mac* [⌘]-[Option]-[K]

Highlight kerning

Windows [Alt]-[→], *Mac* [Option]-[→]

Increase the kerning

This shortcut and the next several change the kerning (the space between two characters) by the increment specified in the Tracking text box on the Type & Auto Tracing sheet of the Preferences dialog box.

Windows [Alt]-[←], *Mac* [Option]-[←]

Decrease the kerning

Windows [Ctrl]-[Alt]-[→], *Mac* [⌘]-[Option]-[→]

Increase the kerning by five times the increment value

Windows [Ctrl]-[Alt]-[←], *Mac* [⌘]-[Option]-[←]

Decrease the kerning by five times the increment value

Windows [Ctrl]-[Alt]-[\], *Mac* [⌘]-[Option]-[\]

Increase the kerning between the selected words by the increment value

Illustrator

Keyboard Shortcuts for Aligning Paragraphs

Windows [Ctrl]-[Shift]-[L], *Mac* [⌘]-[Shift]-[L]
Left-align the paragraph

Windows [Ctrl]-[Shift]-[R], *Mac* [⌘]-[Shift]-[R]
Right-align the paragraph

Windows [Ctrl]-[Shift]-[C], *Mac* [⌘]-[Shift]-[C]
Center the paragraph

Windows [Ctrl]-[Shift]-[J], *Mac* [⌘]-[Shift]-[J]
Justify the paragraph

Working with Palettes

Illustrator's palettes are highly mouse friendly, but you can also perform some actions from the keyboard. Many of the shortcuts for palettes involve pressing one or more keys to modify the mouse action; most don't work (or have different effects) when a Type tool is selected.

Keyboard Shortcuts for Working with All (or Most) Palettes

Windows [Tab], *Mac* [Tab]
Toggle the display of all palettes

Windows [Shift]-[Tab], *Mac* [Shift]-[Tab]
Toggle the display of all palettes except the Toolbox

Windows [Shift]-[Enter], *Mac* [Shift]-[Return]
Apply the value and keep the text box active

Keyboard Shortcuts for Working in the Actions Palette

Windows [Alt]-click the Play button, *Mac* [Option]-click the Play button
Play a single command

Windows [Ctrl]-double-click the Play button,
Mac [⌘]-double-click the Play button

Play the action

Windows [Alt]-click the New Action button,
Mac [Option]-click the
New Action button

Create a new action without displaying the New Action dialog box

Illustrator assigns the new action a default name (for example, Action 1 or Action 2).

Keyboard Shortcuts for Working in the Character and Paragraph Palettes

Windows [↑], *Mac* [↑]

Increase the selected value by a small increment

Windows [↓], *Mac* [↓]

Decrease the selected value by a small increment

Windows [Shift]-[↑], *Mac* [Shift]-[↑]

Increase the selected value by a large increment

Windows [Shift]-[↓], *Mac* [Shift]-[↓]

Decrease the selected value by a large increment

Windows [Ctrl]-[Alt]-[Shift]-[F], *Mac* [⌘]-[Option]-[Shift]-[F]

Select the Font Name field

Keyboard Shortcuts for Working in the Color Palette

Windows [Ctrl]-click the color bar, *Mac* [⌘]-click the color bar

Select the complement for the current color fill or stroke

Windows [Ctrl]-[Alt]-click the color bar, *Mac* [⌘]-[Option]-click the color bar

Select the complement for the nonactive fill or stroke

Illustrator

Windows Alt-click the color bar, *Mac* Option-click the color bar

Change the nonactive fill or stroke

Windows Ctrl-Shift-click the color bar,
Mac ⌘-Shift-click the color bar

Select the inverse for the current fill or stroke

Windows Ctrl-Alt-Shift-click the color bar,
Mac ⌘-Option-Shift-click the color bar

Select the inverse for the nonactive fill or stroke

Windows Shift-click the color bar, *Mac* Shift-click the color bar

Change the color mode

Windows Shift-drag the color slider, *Mac* Shift-drag the color slider

Move the color sliders in tandem

Keyboard Shortcuts for Working in the Layers Palette

Windows Alt-click the layer name, *Mac* Option-click the layer name

Select all objects on the layer

Windows Alt-click the eye icon, *Mac* Option-click the eye icon

Toggle the display of all layers except the selected layer

Windows Ctrl-click the eye icon, *Mac* ⌘-click the eye icon

Toggle between Outline view and Preview for the selected layer

Windows Ctrl-Alt-click the eye icon, *Mac* ⌘-Option-click the eye icon

Toggle between Outline view and Preview for all other layers

Windows Alt-click the expansion triangle,
Mac Option-click the expansion triangle

Expand all sublayers

Windows [Ctrl]-click the New Layer button, *Mac* [⌘]-click the New Layer button

Create a new layer at the top of the layer list

Windows [Ctrl]-[Alt]-click the New Sublayer button,
Mac [⌘]-[Option]-click the New Sublayer button

Create a new sublayer at the bottom of the layer

Windows [Ctrl]-[Alt]-click the New Layer button,
Mac [⌘]-[Option]-click the New Layer button

Create a new layer below the selected layer

Windows [Alt]-drag a selection, *Mac* [Option]-drag a selection

Copy the selection to a new layer, a new sublayer, or a new group

Keyboard Shortcuts for Working in the Swatches Palette

Windows [Ctrl]-click the New Swatch button,
Mac [⌘]-click the New Swatch button

Create a new spot color

Windows [Ctrl]-[Shift]-click the New Swatch button,
Mac [⌘]-[Shift]-click the New Swatch button

Create a new global process color

Windows [Alt]-drag a swatch, *Mac* [Option]-drag a swatch

Replace the swatch on which you drop the swatch you dragged

Windows [Ctrl]-[Alt]-click in the swatch color list,
Mac [⌘]-[Option]-click in the swatch color list

Select the swatch by name

Keyboard Shortcuts for Working in the Transform Palette

Windows [Shift]-[Enter], *Mac* [Shift]-[Return]

Enter the value but leave the focus in the edit field

Illustrator

Windows [Alt]-[Enter], *Mac* [Option]-[Return]

Enter the value and copy the object

Windows [Ctrl]-[Enter], *Mac* [⌘]-[Return]

Enter the value and scale the option proportionately for width or for height

Keyboard Shortcuts for Working in the Transparency Palette

Windows [Alt]-click a mask thumbnail, *Mac* [Option]-click a mask thumbnail

Change the mask to grayscale for editing

Windows [Shift]-click a mask thumbnail, *Mac* [Shift]-click a mask thumbnail

Disable or reenable the opacity mask

Windows [↑], *Mac* [↑]

Increase opacity by 1 percent

Click in the Opacity field before using this shortcut and the next three shortcuts.

Windows [↓], *Mac* [↓]

Decrease opacity by 1 percent

Windows [Shift]-[↑], *Mac* [Shift]-[↑]

Increase opacity by 10 percent

Windows [Shift]-[↓], *Mac* [Shift]-[↓]

Decrease opacity by 10 percent

Customizing Keyboard Shortcuts

Although Illustrator provides many built-in keyboard shortcuts, some menu commands and tools don't have keyboard shortcuts. Illustrator enables you to customize its default keyboard shortcuts and create shortcuts of your own to suit your needs. You can even define multiple sets of keyboard shortcuts so that you can switch from one to another as needed.

To customize keyboard shortcuts, follow these steps:

1. Press [Ctrl]-[Alt]-[Shift]-[K] (on Windows) or [⌘]-[Option]-[Shift]-[K] (on the Mac) or choose Edit | Keyboard Shortcuts to display the Keyboard Shortcuts dialog

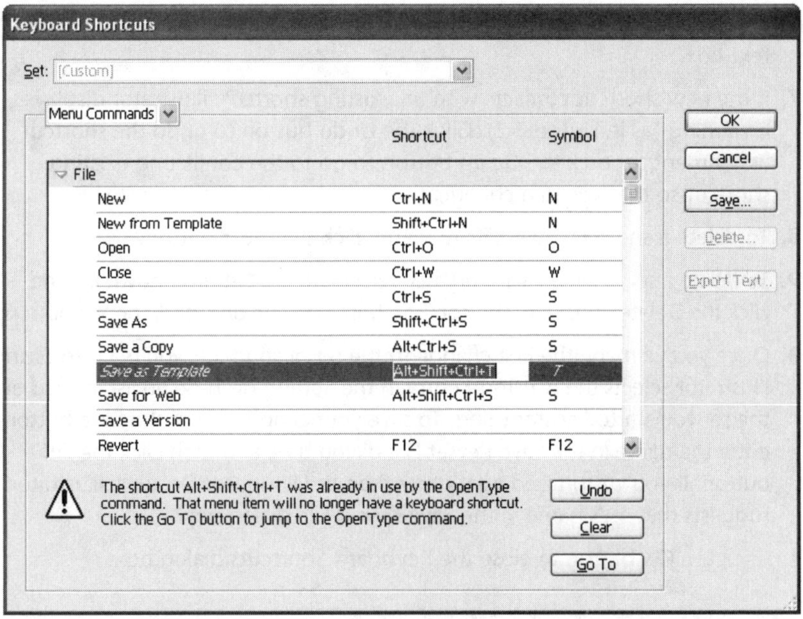

Figure 3-2 *Customize Illustrator's default keyboard shortcuts or create new shortcuts of your own in the Keyboard Shortcuts dialog box.*

box. Figure 3-2 shows the Windows version of the Keyboard Shortcuts dialog box with customization under way.

2. In the Set drop-down list, choose which set of keyboard shortcuts to work with:

- Illustrator starts you off with a set called Illustrator Defaults that contains its default keyboard shortcuts.

- You can create a new set of shortcuts explicitly at this point or wait until you've customized one of the existing sets. To create a new set of shortcuts, click the Save button, type the name for the new set in the Save Keyset File dialog box, and then click the OK button. Illustrator creates the set and selects it in the Set drop-down list.

3. In the drop-down list below the Set drop-down list, select the type of shortcuts you want to work with: Menu Commands or Tools. Illustrator displays the contents of the selected category in the main list box.

4. If you choose Menu Commands in step 3, expand the category of commands you want to work with. For example, expand the File category if you want to work with the commands that appear on the File menu. (If you choose Tools in step 3, you don't need to expand the list of tools, as Illustrator doesn't break it up by category.)

5. Click the command for which you want to create a shortcut or change the existing shortcut. Illustrator displays a selection box in the Shortcut column.

6. Press the keys for the shortcut you want to use. Illustrator enters them in the text box.

7. If the new shortcut conflicts with an existing shortcut, Illustrator displays a warning (as in Figure 3-2). Click the Undo button to undo the shortcut assignment, or click the Go To button to go to the conflicting existing shortcut so that you can change it.

8. To delete a shortcut, select its row and click the Clear button.

9. To delete a set of keyboard shortcuts, select it in the Set drop-down list and click the Delete button. In the confirmation message box, click the Yes button.

10. Once you've made the first change to the set of shortcuts you're customizing, Illustrator selects the [Custom] entry in the Setting drop-down list instead of the set you started customizing. To save your changes, click the Save button, enter the name in the Save Keyset File dialog box, and then click the OK button. If you customized a set other than the Illustrator Defaults, Illustrator suggests that set's name in the Save Keyset File dialog box.

11. Click the OK button to close the Keyboard Shortcuts dialog box.

Automating Tasks in Illustrator

If you find yourself performing the same task repeatedly in Illustrator, consider automating it to save time and work more efficiently. Illustrator offers several features for automating tasks:

- **Actions**   Actions are roughly equivalent to macros in many other applications and provide a quick way for you to show Illustrator which operations you want it to perform. You create an action from the Actions palette by creating a new set, starting the recorder, and recording the sequence of operations needed, usually working on a sample illustration rather than a valuable project. You can then play back the action when necessary. You can also edit an action to change what it does—for example, by adding or removing commands, or by changing the order in which the action executes the commands.

- **Scripts**   Scripts are like actions on steroids, as they can involve not only Illustrator itself but also other applications. Illustrator supports scripts written in Microsoft Visual Basic, AppleScript, and JavaScript, giving plenty of flexibility in both Windows and Mac OS X. You use the File | Scripts submenu to work with scripts.

- **Data-driven graphics**   A data-driven graphic is a means of creating multiple versions of artwork based on the same template. You work in the Variables palette to define those parts of the template that are changeable. For example, you might create a template that included several changeable text strings and linked images. By supplying the data on which text strings and which images to use in different versions of the file, you could then create multiple graphics automatically from the template.

4

Acrobat Keyboard Shortcuts

Acrobat provides keyboard shortcuts for a wide range of operations that you're likely to perform in a day's work—from creating, opening, and saving files through changing the view to activating tools and selecting text. You'll still need to use the mouse at times, but you can get a lot of your work done from the keyboard if you know the right keyboard shortcuts.

Creating, Opening, Saving, Closing, and Printing Files

We'll start (as usual) with the keyboard shortcuts you're almost certain to need: those for creating new files, opening existing files, saving files, closing files, and printing them.

Keyboard Shortcuts for Creating and Opening Files

Windows [Ctrl]-[N], *Mac* [⌘]-[N]

Display the Open dialog box

This shortcut is an alternative to the File | Create PDF | From File command. In the Open dialog box, select the file from which you want to create the PDF file, and then click the Open button. Acrobat creates a new PDF file from the file you specify. Save the file when you're ready.

Windows [Ctrl]-[Shift]-[O], *Mac* [⌘]-[Shift]-[O]

Display the Create PDF From Web Page dialog box

In the Create PDF From Web Page dialog box (the Mac version is shown here), specify the URL of the web page (for example, by typing it or browsing to it), choose suitable settings (for example, whether to get multiple levels, or to get the entire site), and then click the Create button to create a PDF from the page.

Windows [Ctrl]-[O], *Mac* [⌘]-[O]

Display the Open dialog box

Select the file you want to open, and then click the Open button.

Keyboard Shortcuts for Closing and Saving Files, and Quitting Acrobat

Windows [Ctrl]-[W], [Ctrl]-[F4], *Mac* [Ctrl]-[W]

Close the active file

If the file contains unsaved changes, Acrobat prompts you to save them.

Windows [Ctrl]-[S], *Mac* [⌘]-[S]

Save the active file

If the active file hasn't been saved before, Acrobat displays the Save As dialog box so that you can specify the folder and the filename under which to save it. Thereafter, if the file contains unsaved changes, Acrobat saves them under the current filename. If the active file doesn't contain any unsaved changes, the Save command is unavailable, and this keyboard shortcut has no effect.

Windows [Ctrl]-[Shift]-[S], *Mac* [⌘]-[Shift]-[S]

Display the Save As dialog box

Use the Save As dialog box to save the active document under a different name, in a different folder, in a different format, or a combination of the three. When you save in a different format, you can choose further settings by clicking the Settings button and working in the resulting Save As Settings dialog box.

Windows [Ctrl]-[Q], [Alt]-[F4], *Mac* [Ctrl]-[Q]

Quit Acrobat

Keyboard Shortcuts for Displaying Document Properties

Windows `Ctrl`-`D`, *Mac* `⌘`-`D`

Display the Document Properties dialog box

On both Windows and the Mac, you can navigate quickly from category to category in the Document Properties dialog box by pressing `↑` and `↓` or by typing the first letter of the category you want to display: `A` displays the Advanced category, `C` displays the Custom category, and so on.

Keyboard Shortcuts for Page Setup and Printing

Windows `Ctrl`-`Shift`-`P`, *Mac* `⌘`-`Shift`-`P`

Display the Print Setup dialog box

Windows `Ctrl`-`P`, *Mac* `⌘`-`P`

Display the Print dialog box

Windows `Ctrl`-`T`, *Mac* `⌘`-`T`

Issue a Print With Comments command

When you issue a Print With Comments command, Acrobat displays the Summarize Options dialog box (the Windows version is shown here), in which you choose which comments to include, where to print them, and how large to make them. After you click the OK button to close the Summarize Options dialog box, Acrobat displays the Print dialog box.

Acrobat

Windows Ctrl-Alt-P

Display the PrintMe Networks dialog box for Internet printing

Performing Basic Editing Operations

This section discusses the Acrobat shortcuts for performing basic editing operations: Undo and Redo; Cut, Copy, and Paste; finding text; checking spelling; and adding bookmarks.

Keyboard Shortcuts for Undo and Redo

Windows Ctrl-Z, *Mac* ⌘-Z

Undo the last action

Windows Ctrl-Shift-Z, *Mac* ⌘-Shift-Z

Redo the last undone action

Keyboard Shortcuts for Cut, Copy, and Paste

Windows Ctrl-C, *Mac* ⌘-C

Copy the selection

Windows Ctrl-X, *Mac* ⌘-X

Cut the selection

Windows Ctrl-V, *Mac* ⌘-V

Paste the item from the Clipboard

Keyboard Shortcuts for Finding Text

Windows Ctrl-F, *Mac* ⌘-F

Display the Search PDF pane

Windows Ctrl-G, F3, *Mac* ⌘-G

Display the next search result

Windows Ctrl-Shift-G, *Mac* ⌘-Shift-G

Display the previous search result

Windows Ctrl-], *Mac* ⌘-]

Display the next document containing search results

You can use this keyboard shortcut and the next if you choose the All PDF Documents In option button in the Search PDF pane.

Windows Ctrl-[, *Mac* ⌘-[

Display the previous document containing search results

Keyboard Shortcuts for Checking Spelling

Windows F7, *Mac* F7

Check spelling in comments and form fields

Keyboard Shortcuts for Adding Bookmarks

Windows Ctrl-B, *Mac* ⌘-B

Create a bookmark

Acrobat creates a bookmark at the current view and assigns it a default name. Type the name you want the bookmark to have, and then click elsewhere to apply the name.

Selecting Text and Objects

Acrobat provides basic shortcuts for selecting and deselecting all objects, and plenty of shortcuts for selecting text by character, by word, and by line.

Keyboard Shortcuts for Selecting Objects

Windows Ctrl-A, *Mac* ⌘-A

Select all the objects

Windows Ctrl-Shift-A, *Mac* ⌘-Shift-A

Deselect all objects in the current selection

Acrobat

Keyboard Shortcuts for Selecting Text

To select text, activate the Select Text tool, click to place the insertion point, and then use the following keyboard shortcuts.

Windows [Shift]-[←], *Mac* [Shift]-[←]

Extend the selection by one character to the left

> **» Note:** *You can also use these keyboard shortcuts to reduce an existing selection. For example, if you click to place the insertion point and then press* [Shift]-[↓] *to extend the selection downward by one line, you can then press* [Shift]-[←] *to decrease the selection by one character.*

Windows [Shift]-[→], *Mac* [Shift]-[→]

Extend the selection by one character to the right

Windows [Shift]-[↑], *Mac* [Shift]-[↑]

Extend the selection by one line upward

Windows [Shift]-[↓], *Mac* [Shift]-[↓]

Extend the selection by one line downward

Windows [Ctrl]-[Shift]-[←], *Mac* [⌘]-[Shift]-[←]

Extend the selection by one word to the left

Windows [Ctrl]-[Shift]-[→], *Mac* [⌘]-[Shift]-[→]

Extend the selection by one word to the right

Windows [←], *Mac* [←]

Move the insertion point one character to the left

Windows [→], *Mac* [→]

Move the insertion point one character to the right

Windows [↑], *Mac* [↑]

Move the insertion point up one line

Windows [↓], *Mac* [↓]

Move the insertion point down one line

Windows [Ctrl]-[←], *Mac* [⌘]-[←]

Move the insertion point to the beginning of the current word or the previous word

Windows [Ctrl]-[→], *Mac* [⌘]-[→]

Move the insertion point to the end of the current word or the next word

Changing View, Navigating, and Reading Aloud

This section details the keyboard shortcuts that Acrobat provides for the following:

- Changing the view
- Displaying toolbars and moving the focus to them
- Going to views and pages
- Zooming the view
- Rotating the view
- Moving the focus
- Working in the Navigation pane
- Navigating through a document
- Scrolling automatically, and making Acrobat read out loud

Keyboard Shortcuts for Changing the View

Windows [F6], *Mac* [F6]

Toggle the display of the Navigation pane

Windows [F4], *Mac* [F4]

Toggle the display of the How To pane

Windows [Shift]-[F4], *Mac* [Shift]-[F4]

Toggle the focus between the How To pane and the document pane

Windows [Ctrl]-[U], *Mac* [⌘]-[U]

Toggle the display of the grid

Windows [Ctrl]-[Shift]-[U], *Mac* [⌘]-[Shift]-[U]

Toggle the Snap To Grid feature on and off

Acrobat

Windows Ctrl-R, *Mac* ⌘-R

Toggle the display of the rulers

Keyboard Shortcuts for Toolbars

Windows F9, *Mac* F9

Toggle the display of the menu bar

Windows F8, *Mac* F8

Toggle the display of all toolbars

Windows Ctrl-E, *Mac* ⌘-E

Toggle the display of the Properties bar

Windows Ctrl-Alt-D, *Mac* ⌘-Option-D

Dock all toolbars

Windows Alt, then Ctrl-Tab

Move the focus to the toolbar area

After moving the focus to the toolbar area, you can press Ctrl-Tab to move the focus from one toolbar to the next.

Keyboard Shortcuts for Going to Views and Pages

Windows ←, *Mac* ←

Go to the previous page

Windows →, *Mac* →

Go to the next page

Windows Ctrl-Shift-N, *Mac* ⌘-Shift-N

Display the Go To Page dialog box

In the Go To Page dialog box (the Mac version is shown here), type the page number to go to, and then press Enter (on Windows) or Return (on the Mac) to close the dialog box and access that page.

Windows [Alt]-[←], *Mac* [⌘]-[←]

 Go to the previous view

Windows [Alt]-[→], *Mac* [⌘]-[→]

 Go to the next view

Windows [Alt]-[Shift]-[←], *Mac* [⌘]-[Shift]-[←]

 Go to the previous document

Windows [Alt]-[Shift]-[→], *Mac* [⌘]-[Shift]-[→]

 Go to the next document

Keyboard Shortcuts for Zooming the View

Windows [Ctrl]-[+], *Mac* [⌘]-[+]

 Zoom in

Windows [Ctrl]-[-], *Mac* [⌘]-[-]

 Zoom out

Windows [Ctrl]-[Spacebar], then click; *Mac* [⌘]-[Spacebar], then click

 Temporarily select the Zoom In tool

Windows [Ctrl]-[M], *Mac* [⌘]-[M]

 Display the Zoom To dialog box

Use the Zoom To dialog box (the Windows version is shown here) to choose any of the preset zoom percentages (from 6400 percent down to 8.33 percent) or one of the document-related sizes: Actual Size, Fit Page, Fit Width, or Fit Visible. Alternatively, type in the exact zoom percentage you want to use.

Windows [Ctrl]-[0], *Mac* [⌘]-[0]

 Zoom to fit the page

Windows [Ctrl]-[1], *Mac* [⌘]-[1]

 Zoom to actual size

Windows Ctrl-2, *Mac* ⌘-2

Zoom to fit the page width

Windows Ctrl-3, *Mac* ⌘-3

Zoom to fit the visible part of the page

Windows Ctrl-4, *Mac* ⌘-4

Reflow the pages

Keyboard Shortcuts for Rotating the View

Windows Ctrl-Shift-+, *Mac* ⌘-Shift-+

Rotate the view 90 degrees clockwise

Windows Ctrl-Shift--, *Mac* ⌘-Shift--

Rotate the view 90 degrees counterclockwise

Keyboard Shortcuts for Moving the Focus

Windows Tab, →, *Mac* Tab, →

Move the focus to the next field or item in the document pane

Windows Shift-Tab, ←, *Mac* Shift-Tab, ←

Move the focus to the previous field or item in the document pane

Windows Alt-F6

Move the focus to the next floating panel or open dialog box

Keyboard Shortcuts for Working in the Navigation Pane

Windows F6, *Mac* F6

Toggle the display of the Navigation pane

Windows Shift-F6

Toggle the focus between the Navigation pane and the Document pane

Windows Tab, *Mac* Tab

Move the focus to the next element on the selected navigation tab

Press Tab one or more times to select the object you want: the Trash can, the Options menu, the close box, the tab contents, and the tab, in that order.

Windows Shift-Tab, *Mac* ↑

Move the focus to the previous item on the navigation tab

Windows Ctrl-Tab

Make the next tab active

This shortcut works both when the tab itself has the focus and when another part of the Navigation pane has the focus.

Windows Ctrl-Shift-Tab

Make the previous tab active

This shortcut works both when the tab itself has the focus and when another part of the Navigation pane has the focus.

Windows ←

Make the previous tab active

This shortcut works when the focus is on the tab. Because you need to put the focus on the tab manually, usually it's easier to press Ctrl-Tab.

Windows →

Make the next tab active

This shortcut works when the focus is on the tab. Because you need to put the focus on the tab manually, usually it's easier to press Ctrl-Shift-Tab.

Windows →, Shift-+, *Mac* →, Shift-+

Expand the selected bookmark

Windows ←, -, /, *Mac* /

Collapse the selected bookmark

Windows F2, *Mac* F2

Rename the selected bookmark

Acrobat

Keyboard Shortcuts for Navigating Through a Document

Windows ⬆, *Mac* ⬆

Scroll up

Windows ⬇, *Mac* ⬇

Scroll down

Windows [Spacebar], *Mac* [Spacebar]

Scroll

This shortcut works only when the Hand tool is selected.

Windows [Ctrl]-[Shift]-[H], *Mac* [⌘]-[Shift]-[H]

Start or stop automatic scrolling

You can stop automatic scrolling by pressing this shortcut again or (more simply) by pressing [Esc].

Windows [Home], [Ctrl]-[Shift]-[Page Up], [Ctrl]-[Shift]-[⬆],
Mac [Home], [⌘]-[Shift]-[Page Up], [Option]-[Shift]-[⬆]

Display the first page of the document

Windows [End], [Ctrl]-[Shift]-[Page Down], [Ctrl]-[Shift]-[⬇],
Mac [End], [⌘]-[Shift]-[Page Down], [Option]-[Shift]-[⬇]

Display the last page of the document

Windows [Page Down], *Mac* [Page Down]

Display the next screen

Windows [Page Up], *Mac* [Page Up]

Display the previous screen

Keyboard Shortcuts for Reading Out Loud

Windows [Ctrl]-[Shift]-[V], *Mac* [⌘]-[Shift]-[V]

Read the current page aloud

Windows ⌃Ctrl-⇧Shift-Ⓑ, *Mac* ⌘-⇧Shift-Ⓑ

Read from the current selection to the end of the document

Windows ⌃Ctrl-⇧Shift-Ⓒ, *Mac* ⌘-⇧Shift-Ⓒ

Pause reading

Windows ⌃Ctrl-⇧Shift-Ⓔ, *Mac* ⌘-⇧Shift-Ⓔ

Stop reading

Working with Pages

Acrobat provides keyboard shortcuts for inserting new pages, deleting existing pages, cropping pages, and rotating them.

Keyboard Shortcuts for Working with Pages

Windows ⌃Ctrl-⇧Shift-Ⓘ, *Mac* ⌘-⇧Shift-Ⓘ

Display the Select File To Insert dialog box

In the Select File To Insert dialog box, select the file you want to insert, and then click the Select button. In the resulting Insert Pages dialog box (the Mac version is shown here), specify where to locate the pages, and then click the OK button.

Windows ⌃Ctrl-⇧Shift-Ⓓ, *Mac* ⌘-⇧Shift-Ⓓ

Display the Delete Pages dialog box

In the Delete Pages dialog box (the Windows version is shown here), specify the pages to delete, click the OK button, and then click the Yes button in the confirmation dialog box.

Windows [Ctrl]-[Shift]-[T], *Mac* [⌘]-[Shift]-[T]

Display the Crop Pages dialog box

In the Crop Pages dialog box, choose cropping options, and then click the OK button.

Windows [Ctrl]-[Shift]-[R], *Mac* [⌘]-[Shift]-[R]

Display the Rotate Pages dialog box

In the Rotate Pages dialog box (the Mac version is shown here), choose the rotation direction and the pages to rotate, and then click the OK button.

Rotate Pages		
Direction:	Clockwise 90 degrees	
Page Range		
● All		
○ Selection		
○ Pages From:	17 To:	17 of 48
Rotate:	Even and Odd Pages	
	Pages of Any Orientation	
		Cancel OK

Arranging and Closing Windows

Acrobat provides shortcuts for cascading and tiling open windows, closing all windows, toggling full-screen view on and off, and moving quickly from one document to another.

Keyboard Shortcuts for Arranging and Closing Windows

Windows [Ctrl]-[Shift]-[J], *Mac* [⌘]-[Shift]-[J]

Cascade all open windows

Windows [Ctrl]-[Shift]-[K], *Mac* [⌘]-[Shift]-[K]

Tile the open windows horizontally

Windows [Ctrl]-[Shift]-[L], *Mac* [⌘]-[Shift]-[L]

Tile the open windows vertically

Windows [Ctrl]-[Shift]-[W], *Mac* [⌘]-[Shift]-[W]

Close all windows

Windows Ctrl-L, *Mac* ⌘-L

Toggle full-screen view on and off

To turn full-screen view off, you can also press Esc on either Windows or the Mac.

Windows Ctrl-F6, *Mac* ⌘-Shift-~

Activate the next document

This shortcut works only when the focus is on the Document pane.

Selecting Tools

If you work extensively with Acrobat's tools, you can save time and effort by using keyboard shortcuts to select these tools. Before you can do so, however, you must turn on the feature that enables you to use keyboard shortcuts:

1. Press Ctrl-K or choose Edit | Preferences (on Windows), or press ⌘-K or choose Acrobat | Preferences (on the Mac), to display the Preferences dialog box.

2. Press G with the focus in the left list box, or click the General item, to display the General sheet.

3. Select the Use Single-Key Accelerators To Access Tools check box.

4. Click the OK button to close the Preferences dialog box.

Keyboard Shortcuts for Selecting Tools

Windows H, *Mac* H

Select the Hand tool

Windows Spacebar, *Mac* Spacebar

Temporarily select the Hand tool

Windows V, *Mac* V

Select the last selection tool used

The current selection tool is the one selected in the Select drop-down list on the Basic toolbar or the one whose button is selected on the Selection toolbar. This illustration shows the Mac versions of the Basic toolbar and the Selection toolbar.

Windows [Shift]-[V], *Mac* [Shift]-[V]

Cycle through the selection tools

Press this shortcut to revert to the last selection tool used, and then cycle through the other selection tools (the Select Text tool, the Select Image tool, and the Select Table tool, in that order).

Windows [G], *Mac* [G]

Select the Snapshot tool

Windows [Z], *Mac* [Z]

Select the last zoom tool used

The current zoom tool is the tool selected in the Zoom drop-down list.

Windows [Shift]-[Z], *Mac* [Shift]-[Z]

Cycle through the zoom tools

Press this shortcut to revert to the last zoom tool used, and then cycle through the other selection tools (the Zoom In tool, the Zoom Out tool, the Dynamic Zoom tool, and the Loupe, in that order).

Windows [Ctrl]-[Spacebar], *Mac* [⌘]-[Spacebar]

Temporarily select the Zoom In tool

Click to zoom in, or press either [+] (to zoom in) or [-] (to zoom out).

Windows [Shift], *Mac* [Shift]

Temporarily select the Dynamic Zoom tool

This shortcut works only when the Zoom In tool or the Zoom Out tool is selected.

Windows [R], *Mac* [R]

Select the Select Object tool

Windows [A], *Mac* [A]

Select the Article tool

Windows ⒞, *Mac* ⒞

> Select the Crop tool

Windows ⒧, *Mac* ⒧

> Select the Link tool

Windows ⒡, *Mac* ⒡

> Select the current forms tool

Windows Shift-⒡, *Mac* Shift-⒡

> Cycle through the forms tools

Press this shortcut to select the Button tool, the Check Box tool, the Combo Box tool, the List Box tool, the Radio Button tool, the Text Field tool, and the Digital Signature tool in that order, starting from the current forms tool.

Windows ⓜ, *Mac* ⓜ

> Select the Movie tool

Windows Shift-ⓜ, *Mac* Shift-ⓜ

> Select the Sound tool

Windows ⓣ, *Mac* ⓣ

> Select the TouchUp Text tool

Windows Shift-ⓣ, *Mac* Shift-ⓣ

> Select the TouchUp Object tool

Windows ⓑ, *Mac* ⓑ

> Select the Distance tool

Windows Shift-ⓑ, *Mac* Shift-ⓑ

> Cycle through the measuring tools

Press this shortcut to select the Distance tool, the Perimeter tool, and the Area tool in that order, starting from the current measuring tool.

Acrobat

Working with Comments

The keyboard shortcuts that Acrobat provides allow you to perform most of your work with comments by using the keyboard.

Keyboard Shortcuts for Working with Comments

Windows ⟦S⟧, *Mac* ⟦S⟧

Select the Note tool

Windows ⟦E⟧, *Mac* ⟦E⟧

Select the Text Edits tool

Windows ⟦K⟧, *Mac* ⟦K⟧

Select the Stamp tool

Windows ⟦U⟧, *Mac* ⟦U⟧

Select the last highlighting tool used

The last highlighting tool used is the one selected in the Highlighting drop-down list.

Windows ⟦Shift⟧-⟦U⟧, *Mac* ⟦Shift⟧-⟦U⟧

Cycle through the highlighting tools

Press this shortcut to select the Highlighter tool, the Cross-Out Text tool, and the Underline Text tool in that order, starting from the current highlighting tool.

Windows ⟦D⟧, *Mac* ⟦D⟧

Select the last drawing tool

The last drawing tool used is the one selected in the Drawing drop-down list.

Windows ⟦Shift⟧-⟦D⟧, *Mac* ⟦Shift⟧-⟦D⟧

Cycle through the drawing tools

Press this shortcut to select the Rectangle tool, the Oval tool, the Arrow tool, the Line tool, the Cloud tool, the Polygon tool, and the Polygon Line tool in that order, starting from the current tool.

Windows X, *Mac* X

Select the Text Box tool

Windows N, *Mac* N

Select the Pencil tool or the Pencil Eraser tool

This shortcut selects whichever of the Pencil tool or the Pencil Eraser tool was last used.

Windows Shift-N, *Mac* Shift-N

Toggle between the Pencil tool and the Pencil Eraser tool

Windows J, *Mac* J

Select the current attach tool

The current attach tool is the one selected in the Attach drop-down list.

Windows Shift-J, *Mac* Shift-J

Cycle through the attach tools

Press this shortcut to revert to the last attach tool used and then cycle through the attach tools (the Attach File tool, the Attach Sound tool, and the Paste Clipboard Image tool, in that order).

Windows Tab, *Mac* Tab

Move the focus to a comment

Pressing Tab also cycles through form fields in the document.

Windows Spacebar, *Mac* Spacebar

Display a pop-up window for the comment that has the focus

Windows Q, *Mac* Q

Send your comments

Windows O, *Mac* O

Send and receive comments in a browser-based review

Acrobat

Windows ⊞W, Mac ⊞W

Mark the document status as complete in a browser-based review

Windows ⊞Y, Mac ⊞Y

Save the document and work offline in a browser-based review

Windows ⊞I, Mac ⊞I

Go back online

Choosing Advanced Options

Finally, Acrobat provides keyboard shortcuts for displaying the JavaScript debugger, toggling the use of local fonts, and toggling Proof Colors and Overprint Preview.

Keyboard Shortcuts for Choosing Advanced Options

Windows Ctrl-J, Mac ⌘-J

Display the JavaScript debugger

Should you need to debug (troubleshoot) scripts written in JavaScript, this keyboard shortcut can help you quickly reach the debugger.

Windows Ctrl-Shift-Y, Mac ⌘-Shift-Y

Toggle the use of local fonts

Windows Ctrl-Y, Mac ⌘-Y

Toggle Proof Colors on and off

Windows Ctrl-Alt-Shift-Y, Mac ⌘-Option-Shift-Y

Toggle Overprint Preview on and off

Use Overprint Preview to get an idea, on screen, of how overprints will turn out on paper.

5

InDesign Keyboard Shortcuts

To help you lay out your documents quickly, InDesign provides a wide range of keyboard shortcuts. This chapter starts with the shortcuts for creating, opening, saving, and closing documents; continues with shortcuts for performing standard editing operations, changing the view, and navigating in a document; meanders through working with type and text, objects, and tables; and finally arrives at selecting tools. The chapter finishes by showing you how to customize InDesign's default keyboard shortcuts and create shortcuts of your own.

Creating, Opening, Saving, and Closing Documents

InDesign supports largely standard keyboard shortcuts for creating new files, opening and closing files, and saving them. InDesign offers extra keyboard shortcuts for Save As and Save A Copy operations, for importing and exporting files, and for preflight checks and packaging.

Keyboard Shortcuts for Creating New Files

Windows Ctrl-N, *Mac* ⌘-N

Display the New Document dialog box

Use the options in the New Document dialog box to specify the number of pages, page size, orientation, columns, margins, and other details for the document you want to create.

Windows Ctrl-Alt-P, *Mac* ⌘-Option-P

Display the Document Setup dialog box

Use the Document Setup dialog box (the Mac version is shown here) to change the setup of the document you're working on.

Document Setup

Number of Pages: 1   ☑ Facing Pages
                      ☐ Master Text Frame

                                      OK
                                      Cancel
                                      Fewer Options

Page Size: Letter

Width: ⬍ 51p0   Orientation: ▣ ▣
Height: ⬍ 66p0

Bleed and Slug

          Top   Bottom   Inside   Outside
Bleed: 0p0   0p0   0p0   0p0   ⬙
Slug: 0p0   0p0   0p0   0p0   ⬙

Windows ⌨Ctrl⌨-⌨O⌨, *Mac* ⌨⌘⌨-⌨O⌨

Display the Open A File dialog box

The Open A File dialog box works like a standard Open
dialog box except that it also enables you to choose
whether to open the file as a normal file, as an original,
or as a copy by selecting the appropriate option button:

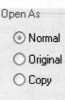

Open As
⦿ Normal
◯ Original
◯ Copy

Windows ⌨Ctrl⌨-⌨W⌨, *Mac* ⌨⌘⌨-⌨W⌨

Close the active file

If the active file contains unsaved changes, InDesign prompts you to save it.

Keyboard Shortcuts for Saving Files

Windows ⌨Ctrl⌨-⌨S⌨, *Mac* ⌨⌘⌨-⌨S⌨

Save the active file

The first time you save a file, InDesign displays the Save As dialog box so that you
can specify the filename, the folder, and the format to use. Thereafter, when you
issue a Save command, InDesign saves the file under its existing name without
displaying the Save As dialog box.

Windows Ctrl-Shift-S, *Mac* ⌘-Shift-S

Display the Save As dialog box

Use the Save As dialog box when you need to save the active file under a different name, in a different location, in a different format, or a combination of the three.

Windows Ctrl-Alt-S, *Mac* ⌘-Option-S

Display the Save A Copy dialog box

Use the Save A Copy dialog box to save an identical copy of the active file but to leave the original file active. (By contrast, using a Save As command leaves the new file active.) By saving a copy, you can preserve the intermediate stages of your work without interrupting its flow.

Keyboard Shortcuts for Importing and Exporting Files

Windows Ctrl-D, *Mac* ⌘-D

Display the Place dialog box

Windows Ctrl-E, *Mac* ⌘-E

Display the Export dialog box

Keyboard Shortcuts for Preflight, Package, and Print

Windows Ctrl-Alt-Shift-F, *Mac* ⌘-Option-Shift-F

Display the Preflight dialog box

Use the Preflight dialog box to quality-check a document or book before printing it or sending it to a service bureau.

Windows Ctrl-Alt-Shift-P, *Mac* ⌘-Option-Shift-P

Start the process of packaging the active document or book

Windows Ctrl-P, *Mac* ⌘-P

Display the Print dialog box

Performing Standard Editing Operations

InDesign offers keyboard shortcuts for standard editing operations such as undo and redo; Paste Into and Paste In Place operations as well as the standard Cut, Copy, and Paste operations; toggling between the Story Editor and Layout; finding text and checking spelling; and configuring InDesign.

Keyboard Shortcuts for Undo and Redo

Windows [Ctrl]-[Z], *Mac* [⌘]-[Z]

Undo the last operation

InDesign enables you to undo multiple operations and redo the operations you've undone.

Windows [Ctrl]-[Shift]-[Z], *Mac* [⌘]-[Shift]-[Z]

Redo the last undone operation

Keyboard Shortcuts for Cut, Copy, and Paste

Windows [Ctrl]-[X], *Mac* [⌘]-[X]

Cut

Windows [Ctrl]-[C], *Mac* [⌘]-[C]

Copy

Windows [Ctrl]-[V], *Mac* [⌘]-[V]

Paste

Windows [Ctrl]-[Alt]-[V], *Mac* [⌘]-[Option]-[V]

Paste into the selection

Windows [Ctrl]-[Alt]-[Shift]-[V], *Mac* [⌘]-[Option]-[Shift]-[V]

Paste In Place

Use the Paste In Place command to position the item you're pasting to appear at the same page coordinates as the original item.

Keyboard Shortcuts for Toggling Between the Story Editor and Layout

Windows [Ctrl]-[Y], *Mac* [⌘]-[Y]

Toggle between the Story Editor and Layout

Select the item you want to edit, and then press this shortcut to edit it in the Story Editor. Press this shortcut again to return to Layout when you've finished editing.

Keyboard Shortcuts for Finding Text and Checking Spelling

Windows [Ctrl]-[F], *Mac* [⌘]-[F]

Display the Find/Change dialog box

Windows [Ctrl]-[Alt]-[F], [Shift]-[F2], *Mac* [⌘]-[Option]-[F], [Shift]-[F2]

Find the next instance of the current search string

Press this shortcut to find the next instance of the current search string (the last string of text you searched for) without displaying the Find/Change dialog box.

Windows [Ctrl]-[F1], *Mac* [⌘]-[F1]

Insert the selected text in the Find What text box

For this shortcut and the next, display the Find/Change dialog box before pressing the shortcut.

Windows [Ctrl]-[F2], *Mac* [⌘]-[F2]

Insert the selected text in the Change To text box

Windows [Ctrl]-[F3], *Mac* [⌘]-[F3]

Replace the selection with the text in the Change To text box

Windows [Ctrl]-[I], *Mac* [⌘]-[I]

Display the Check Spelling dialog box

Keyboard Shortcuts for Configuring InDesign

Windows [Ctrl]-[K], *Mac* [⌘]-[K]

Display the Preferences dialog box

Windows ⌨Ctrl⌨-⌨Alt⌨-⌨Shift⌨-⌨U⌨, *Mac* ⌨⌘⌨-⌨Option⌨-⌨Shift⌨-⌨U⌨

Cycle through the units of measurement

If you have the rulers displayed, you'll see the units change on them.

Changing the View

This section details the keyboard shortcuts that InDesign offers for navigating among windows, zooming the view, displaying and hiding on-screen items and palettes, using Overprint Preview and the Separations Preview palette, and changing display performance.

Keyboard Shortcuts for Navigating Among Windows

Windows ⌨Ctrl⌨-⌨F6⌨, ⌨Ctrl⌨-⌨~⌨, *Mac* ⌨⌘⌨-⌨F6⌨, ⌨⌘⌨-⌨~⌨

Switch to the next window

Windows ⌨Ctrl⌨-⌨Shift⌨-⌨F6⌨, ⌨Ctrl⌨-⌨Shift⌨-⌨~⌨, *Mac* ⌨⌘⌨-⌨Shift⌨-⌨F6⌨, ⌨⌘⌨-⌨Shift⌨-⌨~⌨

Switch to the previous window

Keyboard Shortcuts for Zooming the View

Windows ⌨Ctrl⌨-⌨=⌨, *Mac* ⌨⌘⌨-⌨=⌨

Zoom in by one preset zoom increment

Windows ⌨Ctrl⌨-⌨-⌨, *Mac* ⌨⌘⌨-⌨-⌨

Zoom out by one preset zoom increment

Windows ⌨Ctrl⌨-⌨0⌨, *Mac* ⌨⌘⌨-⌨0⌨

Zoom to fit the page in the window

Windows ⌨Ctrl⌨-⌨Alt⌨-⌨0⌨, *Mac* ⌨⌘⌨-⌨Option⌨-⌨0⌨

Zoom to fit the spread in the window

Windows ⌨Ctrl⌨-⌨1⌨, *Mac* ⌨⌘⌨-⌨1⌨

Zoom to the document's actual size

InDesign

Windows Ctrl-5, *Mac* ⌘-5

    Zoom to 50 percent zoom

Windows Ctrl-2, *Mac* ⌘-2

    Zoom to 200 percent zoom

Windows Ctrl-4, *Mac* ⌘-4

    Zoom to 400 percent zoom

Windows Ctrl-Alt-5, *Mac* ⌘-Option-5

    Select the Zoom field

    Type the zoom percentage you want, and then press Enter (on Windows) or Return (on the Mac).

Windows Ctrl-Alt-Shift-0, *Mac* ⌘-Option-Shift-0

    Zoom to fit the entire pasteboard in the window

Windows Ctrl-Alt-+, *Mac* ⌘-Option-+

    Zoom to fit the current selection in the window

Windows Ctrl-Alt-2, *Mac* ⌘-Option-2

    Toggle between the current zoom percentage and the previous zoom percentage

Windows Ctrl-Spacebar, *Mac* ⌘-Spacebar

    Temporarily select the Zoom In tool

Windows Ctrl-Alt-Spacebar, *Mac* ⌘-Option-Spacebar

    Temporarily select the Zoom Out tool

    You can also temporarily select the Zoom Out tool by pressing Alt (on Windows) or Option (on the Mac) while the Zoom In tool is selected.

Keyboard Shortcuts for Displaying and Hiding Items

Windows Ctrl-Alt-1, *Mac* ⌘-Option-1

    Toggle the display of the document's structure

Windows Ctrl-Alt-Y, *Mac* ⌘-Option-Y
Toggle the display of text threads

Windows Ctrl-H, *Mac* ⌘-H
Toggle the display of frame edges

Windows Ctrl-R, *Mac* ⌘-R
Toggle the display of rulers

Windows Ctrl-;, *Mac* ⌘-;
Toggle the display of guides

Windows Ctrl-Alt-;, *Mac* ⌘-Option-;
Toggle locking on guides

Windows Ctrl-Shift-;, *Mac* ⌘-Shift-;
Toggle the Snap To Guides feature on and off

Windows Ctrl-Alt-G, *Mac* ⌘-Option-G
Select all guides

Windows Ctrl-Alt-", *Mac* ⌘-Option-"
Toggle the display of the baseline grid

Windows Ctrl-', *Mac* ⌘-'
Toggle the display of the document grid

Windows Ctrl-Shift-', *Mac* ⌘-Shift-'
Toggle the Snap To Document Grid feature on and off

Keyboard Shortcuts for Displaying and Hiding Palettes

The following keyboard shortcuts let you quickly activate, display, and hide the palettes you need. When a palette has only one tab, the keyboard shortcut acts as a toggle: if the palette is displayed, pressing the keyboard shortcut hides the palette; and if the palette is hidden, pressing the keyboard shortcut displays it. When a palette has multiple tabs, pressing the keyboard shortcut:

- Displays the palette if it's hidden
- Activates the palette if it's displayed but one of the other tabs is active
- Hides the palette if it's displayed and active

Windows [Shift]-[F7], *Mac* [Shift]-[F7]

Activate or toggle the display of the Align palette

Windows [F6], *Mac* [F6]

Toggle the display of the Color palette

Windows [Ctrl]-[Alt]-[6], *Mac* [⌘]-[Option]-[6]

Toggle the display of the Control palette

Windows [Ctrl]-[6], *Mac* [⌘]-[6]

Toggle the focus to and from the Control palette

Press this shortcut to quickly move the focus to the Control palette. Press this shortcut again to return the focus to where it was before.

Windows [F8], *Mac* [F8]

Activate or toggle the display of the Info palette

Windows [F7], *Mac* [F7]

Activate or toggle the display of the Layers palette

Windows [Ctrl]-[Shift]-[D], *Mac* [⌘]-[Shift]-[D]

Toggle the display of the Links palette

Windows [Shift]-[F6], *Mac* [Shift]-[F6]

Activate or toggle the display of the Separations Preview palette

Windows [F12], *Mac* [F12]

Activate or toggle the display of the Pages palette

Windows F10, *Mac* F10

Activate or toggle the display of the Stroke palette

» Caution: *On Mac OS X version 10.3 (Panther), the* F9*,* F10*, and* F11 *keyboard shortcuts are assigned to the Exposé feature by default. Pressing* Shift *with one of these shortcuts (for example,* Shift*-*F9*) slows down the effect of the Exposé animation. So you can't use any of these keyboard shortcuts—*F9*,* Shift*-*F9*,* F10*,* Shift*-*F10*,* F11*, or* Shift*-*F11*—in InDesign unless you reassign the Exposé keyboard shortcuts. To reassign them, open System Preferences and work on the Exposé sheet.*

Windows F5, *Mac* F5

Activate or toggle the display of the Swatches palette

Windows F9, *Mac* F9

Activate or toggle the display of the Transform palette

Windows Shift-F10, *Mac* Shift-F10

Activate or toggle the display of the Transparency palette

Windows Ctrl-T, *Mac* ⌘-T

Activate or toggle the display of the Character palette

Windows Ctrl-Alt-T, *Mac* ⌘-Option-T

Activate or toggle the display of the Paragraph palette

Windows F11, *Mac* F11

Activate or toggle the display of the Paragraph Styles palette

Windows Shift-F11, *Mac* Shift-F11

Activate or toggle the display of the Character Styles palette

Windows Shift-F8, *Mac* Shift-F8

Toggle the display of the Index palette

Windows Ctrl-Shift-T, *Mac* ⌘-Shift-T

Activate or toggle the display of the Tabs palette

Windows [Shift]-[F9], *Mac* [Shift]-[F9]

Toggle the display of the Table palette

Windows [Ctrl]-[Alt]-[W], *Mac* [⌘]-[Option]-[W]

Toggle the display of the Text Wrap palette

Keyboard Shortcuts for Overprint Preview and Separations Preview

Windows [Ctrl]-[Alt]-[Shift]-[Y], *Mac* [⌘]-[Option]-[Shift]-[Y]

Toggle Overprint Preview on and off

Windows [Ctrl]-[Alt]-[Shift]-[~], *Mac* [⌘]-[Option]-[Shift]-[~]

Show all plates

>> Note: *You must turn on Separations Preview (press* [Shift]-[F6]*) before you can use the following keyboard shortcuts.*

Windows [Ctrl]-[Alt]-[Shift]-[1], *Mac* [⌘]-[Option]-[Shift]-[1]

Show the Cyan plate

Windows [Ctrl]-[Alt]-[Shift]-[2], *Mac* [⌘]-[Option]-[Shift]-[2]

Show the Magenta plate

Windows [Ctrl]-[Alt]-[Shift]-[3], *Mac* [⌘]-[Option]-[Shift]-[3]

Show the Yellow plate

Windows [Ctrl]-[Alt]-[Shift]-[4], *Mac* [⌘]-[Option]-[Shift]-[4]

Show the Black plate

Windows [Ctrl]-[Alt]-[Shift]-[5], *Mac* [⌘]-[Option]-[Shift]-[5]

Show the 1st Spot plate

Windows [Ctrl]-[Alt]-[Shift]-[6], *Mac* [⌘]-[Option]-[Shift]-[6]

Show the 2nd Spot plate

Windows [Ctrl]-[Alt]-[Shift]-[7], *Mac* [⌘]-[Option]-[Shift]-[7]

Show the 3rd Spot plate

InDesign

Windows `Ctrl`-`Alt`-`Shift`-`8`, *Mac* `⌘`-`Option`-`Shift`-`8`

Show the 4th Spot plate

Windows `Ctrl`-`Alt`-`Shift`-`9`, *Mac* `⌘`-`Option`-`Shift`-`9`

Show the 5th Spot plate

Keyboard Shortcuts for Changing Display Performance

Windows `Ctrl`-`Alt`-`O`, *Mac* `⌘`-`Option`-`O`

Set the display performance to Optimized

Windows `Ctrl`-`Alt`-`Z`, *Mac* `⌘`-`Option`-`Z`

Set the display performance to Typical

Windows `Ctrl`-`Alt`-`H`, *Mac* `⌘`-`Option`-`H`

Set the display performance to High Quality

Navigating in a Document

InDesign provides keyboard shortcuts for navigating quickly from page to page in a document and for navigating in XML.

Keyboard Shortcuts for Navigating in a Document

Windows `Ctrl`-`Shift`-`Page Up`, *Mac* `⌘`-`Shift`-`Page Up`

Go to the first page in the document

Windows `Ctrl`-`Shift`-`Page Down`, *Mac* `⌘`-`Shift`-`Page Down`

Go to the last page in the document

Windows `Shift`-`Page Up`, *Mac* `Shift`-`Page Up`

Go to the previous page

Windows `Shift`-`Page Down`, *Mac* `Shift`-`Page Down`

Go to the next page

Windows `Alt`-`Page Up`, *Mac* `Option`-`Page Up`

Go to the previous spread

Windows [Alt]-[Page Down], *Mac* [Option]-[Page Down]

Go to the next spread

Windows [Ctrl]-[Page Up], *Mac* [⌘]-[Page Up]

Go back to the last page you worked on

Windows [Ctrl]-[Page Down], *Mac* [⌘]-[Page Down]

Go forward again after going back

Windows [Ctrl]-[J], *Mac* [⌘]-[J]

Select the page number in the page box

Type the number of the page you want to move to, and then press [Enter] (on Windows) or [Return] (on the Mac).

Keyboard Shortcuts for Navigating in XML

Windows [→], *Mac* [→]

Expand the selected element

Windows [←], *Mac* [←]

Collapse the selected element

Windows [Alt]-[→], *Mac* [Option]-[→]

Expand the selected element and its child elements

Windows [Alt]-[←], *Mac* [Option]-[←]

Collapse the selected element and its child elements

Windows [Shift]-[↑], *Mac* [Shift]-[↑]

Extend the XML selection up

Windows [Shift]-[↓], *Mac* [Shift]-[↓]

Extend the XML selection down

Windows [↑], *Mac* [↑]

Move the XML selection up

Windows ⬇, *Mac* ⬇

Move the XML selection down

Windows Page Down, *Mac* Page Down

Scroll the structure pane down one screen

Windows Page Up, *Mac* Page Up

Scroll the structure pane up one screen

Windows Home, *Mac* Home

Select the first XML node

Windows End, *Mac* End

Select the last XML node

Windows Shift-Home, *Mac* Shift-Home

Extend the selection to the first XML node

Windows Shift-End, *Mac* Shift-End

Extend the selection to the last XML node

Windows Ctrl-➡, *Mac* ⌘-➡

Go to the next validation error

Windows Ctrl-⬅, *Mac* ⌘-⬅

Go to the previous validation error

Working with Type and Text

If you're laying out documents with InDesign, you'll probably spend a lot of time working with type and text. This section lists the keyboard shortcuts that InDesign offers for many of the operations you'll want to perform with type and text, from navigating through text to creating index entries.

Keyboard Shortcuts for Navigating Through Text

Windows ⬅, *Mac* ⬅

    Move to the left by one character

Windows ➡, *Mac* ➡

    Move to the right by one character

Windows ⬆, *Mac* ⬆

    Move up one line

Windows ⬇, *Mac* ⬇

    Move down one line

Windows Ctrl-⬅, *Mac* ⌘-⬅

    Move one word to the left

Windows Ctrl-➡, *Mac* ⌘-➡

    Move one word to the right

Windows Home, *Mac* Home

    Move to the start of the line

Windows End, *Mac* End

    Move to the end of the line

Windows Ctrl-Home, *Mac* ⌘-Home

    Move to the start of the story

Windows Ctrl-End, *Mac* ⌘-End

    Move to the end of the story

Windows `Ctrl`-`↑`, *Mac* `⌘`-`↑`

Move to the previous paragraph

Windows `Ctrl`-`↓`, *Mac* `⌘`-`↓`

Move to the next paragraph

Keyboard Shortcuts for Selecting Text

Windows `Shift`-`←`, *Mac* `Shift`-`←`

Select one character to the left

Windows `Shift`-`→`, *Mac* `Shift`-`→`

Select one character to the right

Windows `Shift`-`↑`, *Mac* `Shift`-`↑`

Select one line up

Windows `Shift`-`↓`, *Mac* `Shift`-`↓`

Select one line down

Windows `Shift`-`Home`, *Mac* `Shift`-`Home`

Select from the insertion point to the start of the line

Windows `Shift`-`End`, *Mac* `Shift`-`End`

Select from the insertion point to the end of the line

Windows `Ctrl`-`Shift`-`↑`, *Mac* `⌘`-`Shift`-`↑`

Select one paragraph up

Windows `Ctrl`-`Shift`-`↓`, *Mac* `⌘`-`Shift`-`↓`

Select one paragraph down

Windows `Ctrl`-`Shift`-`\`, *Mac* `⌘`-`Shift`-`\`

Select the current line

Windows Shift-click, *Mac* Shift-click

Select from the insertion point to where you click

Windows Ctrl-Shift-Home, *Mac* ⌘-Shift-Home

Select from the insertion point to the start of the story

Windows Ctrl-Shift-End, *Mac* ⌘-Shift-End

Select from the insertion point to the end of the story

Windows Ctrl-A, *Mac* ⌘-A

Select all the current story

Keyboard Shortcuts for Working with Text

Windows Ctrl-Shift-B, *Mac* ⌘-Shift-B

Toggle boldface

Windows Ctrl-Shift-I, *Mac* ⌘-Shift-I

Toggle italic

Windows Ctrl-Shift-Y, *Mac* ⌘-Shift-Y

Toggle normal formatting

Windows Ctrl-Shift-U, *Mac* ⌘-Shift-U

Toggle underline

Windows Ctrl-Shift-/, *Mac* ⌘-Shift-/

Toggle strikethrough

Windows Ctrl-Shift-K, *Mac* ⌘-Shift-K

Toggle small caps

Windows Ctrl-Shift-+, *Mac* ⌘-Shift-+

Toggle superscript

InDesign

Windows Ctrl-Alt-Shift-+, *Mac* ⌘-Option-Shift-+

Toggle subscript

Windows Ctrl-Shift-X, *Mac* ⌘-Shift-X

Reset the horizontal scale to 100 percent

Windows Ctrl-Alt-Shift-X, *Mac* ⌘-Option-Shift-X

Reset the vertical scale to 100 percent

Windows Ctrl-Alt-Shift-", *Mac* ⌘-Option-Shift-"

Toggle the Use Typographer's Quotes setting

This setting appears on the Text sheet of the Preferences dialog box.

Windows Ctrl-Alt-Shift-G, *Mac* ⌘-Option-Shift-G

Toggle aligning to grid on and off

Windows Ctrl-Alt-Shift-N, *Mac* ⌘-Option-Shift-N

Automatically insert the current page number

Windows Ctrl-Alt-Shift-/, *Mac* ⌘-Option-Shift-/

Update the missing font list

Windows Ctrl-Shift-P, *Mac* ⌘-Shift-P

Add a new page after the last page

Windows Ctrl-Alt-Shift-L, *Mac* ⌘-Option-Shift-L

Override all master page items for the current spread

Keyboard Shortcuts for Working with Character and Paragraph Styles

Windows Ctrl-Alt-Shift-C, *Mac* ⌘-Option-Shift-C

Make the character style definition match the selected text

Windows Ctrl-Alt-Shift-R, *Mac* ⌘-Option-Shift-R

Make the paragraph style definition match the selected text

Windows Ctrl-Alt-Shift-click the style,
  Mac ⌘-Option-Shift-click the style

Change options but don't apply the style

Windows Alt-click the paragraph style name,
  Mac Option-click the paragraph style name

Remove the style and local formatting

Windows Alt-Shift-click the paragraph style name,
  Mac Option-Shift-click the paragraph style name

Clear overrides from the paragraph style

Keyboard Shortcuts for Changing Point Size and Leading

These shortcuts use the increment set in the Size/Leading text box on the Units & Increments sheet of the Preferences dialog box (Ctrl-K on Windows, ⌘-K on the Mac).

Windows Ctrl-Shift->, *Mac* ⌘-Shift->

Increase the point size by one increment

Windows Ctrl-Shift-<, *Mac* ⌘-Shift-<

Decrease the point size by one increment

Windows Ctrl-Alt-Shift->, *Mac* ⌘-Option-Shift->

Increase the point size by five increments

Windows Ctrl-Alt-Shift-<, *Mac* ⌘-Option-Shift-<

Decrease the point size by five increments

Windows Alt-↑, *Mac* Option-↑

Decrease the leading on horizontal text by one increment

Windows Alt-↓, *Mac* Option-↓

Increase the leading on horizontal text by one increment

Windows Alt-→, *Mac* Option-→

Increase the leading on vertical text by one increment

Windows Alt-←, *Mac* Option-←

Decrease the leading on vertical text by one increment

Windows Ctrl-Alt-↑, *Mac* ⌘-Option-↑

Decrease the leading on horizontal text by five increments

Windows Ctrl-Alt-↓, *Mac* ⌘-Option-↓

Increase the leading on horizontal text by five increments

Windows Ctrl-Alt-→, *Mac* ⌘-Option-→

Increase the leading on vertical text by five increments

Windows Ctrl-Alt-←, *Mac* ⌘-Option-←

Decrease the leading on vertical text by five increments

Windows Ctrl-Alt-Shift-A, *Mac* ⌘-Option-Shift-A

Toggle automatic leading on and off

Keyboard Shortcuts for Kerning and Baseline Shift

These shortcuts use the increment set in the Size/Leading text box on the Units & Increments sheet of the Preferences dialog box (Ctrl-K on Windows, ⌘-K on the Mac).

Windows Alt-→, *Mac* Option-→

Increase the kerning on horizontal text by one increment

Windows Alt-←, *Mac* Option-←

Decrease the kerning on horizontal text by one increment

Windows Alt-↓, *Mac* Option-↓

Increase the kerning on vertical text by one increment

Windows [Alt]-[↑], *Mac* [Option]-[↑]

Decrease the kerning on vertical text by one increment

Windows [Ctrl]-[Alt]-[↑], *Mac* [⌘]-[Option]-[↑]

Decrease the kerning on vertical text by five increments

Windows [Ctrl]-[Alt]-[↓], *Mac* [⌘]-[Option]-[↓]

Increase the kerning on vertical text by five increments

Windows [Ctrl]-[Alt]-[→], *Mac* [⌘]-[Option]-[→]

Increase the kerning on horizontal text by five increments

Windows [Ctrl]-[Alt]-[←], *Mac* [⌘]-[Option]-[←]

Decrease the kerning on horizontal text by five increments

Windows [Ctrl]-[Alt]-[\], *Mac* [⌘]-[Option]-[\]

Increase the kerning between words by one increment

Windows [Ctrl]-[Alt]-[Backspace], *Mac* [⌘]-[Option]-[Delete]

Decrease the kerning between words by one increment

Windows [Ctrl]-[Alt]-[Shift]-[\], *Mac* [⌘]-[Option]-[Shift]-[\]

Increase the kerning between words by five increments

Windows [Ctrl]-[Alt]-[Shift]-[Backspace], *Mac* [⌘]-[Option]-[Shift]-[Delete]

Decrease the kerning between words by five increments

Windows [Ctrl]-[Alt]-[Q], *Mac* [⌘]-[Option]-[Q]

Clear all manual kerning and reset tracking to zero

Windows [Alt]-[Shift]-[↑], *Mac* [Option]-[Shift]-[↑]

Increase the baseline shift on horizontal text by one increment

Windows [Alt]-[Shift]-[↓], *Mac* [Option]-[Shift]-[↓]

Decrease the baseline shift on horizontal text by one increment

Windows Alt-Shift-→, *Mac* Option-Shift-→

Increase the baseline shift on vertical text by one increment

Windows Alt-Shift-←, *Mac* Option-Shift-←

Decrease the baseline shift on vertical text by one increment

Windows Ctrl-Alt-Shift-↑, *Mac* ⌘-Option-Shift-↑

Increase the baseline shift on horizontal text by five increments

Windows Ctrl-Alt-Shift-↓, *Mac* ⌘-Option-Shift-↓

Decrease the baseline shift on horizontal text by five increments

Windows Ctrl-Alt-Shift-→, *Mac* ⌘-Option-Shift-→

Increase the baseline shift on vertical text by five increments

Windows Ctrl-Alt-Shift-←, *Mac* ⌘-Option-Shift-←

Decrease the baseline shift on vertical text by five increments

Keyboard Shortcuts for Flowing and Recomposing

Windows Shift-click the loaded text icon,
Mac Shift-click the loaded text icon

Flow the story automatically

In automatic flowing, InDesign automatically adds pages and frames as needed to flow all the text into the document.

Windows Alt-click the loaded text icon,
Mac Option-click the loaded text icon

Flow the story semiautomatically

In semiautomatic flowing, InDesign automatically reloads the loaded text icon for you (so that you don't have to load it manually), but you get to control the flow from frame to frame.

Windows Ctrl-Alt-/, *Mac* ⌘-Option-/

Recompose all stories

Keyboard Shortcuts for Aligning Paragraphs

Windows Ctrl-Shift-L, *Mac* ⌘-Shift-L
   Align left

Windows Ctrl-Shift-C, *Mac* ⌘-Shift-C
   Center the paragraph

Windows Ctrl-Shift-R, *Mac* ⌘-Shift-R
   Align right

Windows Ctrl-Shift-J, *Mac* ⌘-Shift-J
   Justify all lines except the last line

Windows Ctrl-Shift-F, *Mac* ⌘-Shift-F
   Justify all lines, including the last line (forced justification)

Keyboard Shortcuts for Working with Type

Windows Ctrl-Alt-Shift-J, *Mac* ⌘-Option-Shift-J
   Display the Justification dialog box

Windows Ctrl-Alt-J, *Mac* ⌘-Option-J
   Display the Paragraph Rules dialog box

Windows Ctrl-Alt-K, *Mac* ⌘-Option-K
   Display the Keep Options dialog box

Windows Ctrl-Shift-O, *Mac* ⌘-Shift-O
   Create outlines from the selected text

Windows Ctrl-Alt-I, *Mac* ⌘-Option-I
   Toggle the display of hidden characters

Keyboard Shortcuts for Creating Index Entries

Windows ⌈Ctrl⌉-⌈U⌉, *Mac* ⌈⌘⌉-⌈U⌉

Display the New Page Reference dialog box

Windows ⌈Ctrl⌉-⌈Alt⌉-⌈U⌉, *Mac* ⌈⌘⌉-⌈Option⌉-⌈U⌉

Create an index entry without displaying the New Page Reference dialog box

Windows ⌈Ctrl⌉-⌈Shift⌉-⌈F8⌉, *Mac* ⌈⌘⌉-⌈Shift⌉-⌈F8⌉

Create a proper-name index entry

A proper-name index entry has the form *Lastname, Firstname*—for example, Sixpack, Jill.

Working with Objects

InDesign includes keyboard shortcuts for selecting objects and performing a wide variety of operations on them, from duplicating, moving, and grouping them to working with frames, drop shadows, and paths.

Keyboard Shortcuts for Selecting Objects

Windows ⌈Ctrl⌉-⌈A⌉, *Mac* ⌈⌘⌉-⌈A⌉

Select all objects

Windows ⌈Ctrl⌉-⌈Shift⌉-⌈A⌉, *Mac* ⌈⌘⌉-⌈Shift⌉-⌈A⌉

Deselect all objects

Windows ⌈Ctrl⌉-⌈Alt⌉-⌈]⌉, *Mac* ⌈⌘⌉-⌈Option⌉-⌈]⌉

Select the next object above the current object

Windows ⌈Ctrl⌉-⌈Alt⌉-click, *Mac* ⌈⌘⌉-⌈Option⌉-click

Select the next object above the current object

This shortcut works when the Selection tool is selected.

Windows ⌈Ctrl⌉-⌈Alt⌉-⌈[⌉, *Mac* ⌈⌘⌉-⌈Option⌉-⌈[⌉

Select the next object below the current object

Windows [Ctrl]-click, *Mac* [⌘]-click

Select the next object below the current object

This shortcut works when the Selection tool is selected.

Windows [Shift]-click, *Mac* [Shift]-click

Add an object to or remove an object from the selection

This shortcut works when the Selection tool, the Direct Selection tool, or the Group Selection tool is selected.

Windows [Ctrl]-[Shift]-click, *Mac* [⌘]-[Shift]-click

Select the master page item from the document page

This shortcut works when the Selection tool or the Direct Selection tool is selected.

Windows [Ctrl]-[Alt]-[Page Up], *Mac* [⌘]-[Option]-[Page Up]

Select the previous frame in the story

Windows [Ctrl]-[Alt]-[Page Down], *Mac* [⌘]-[Option]-[Page Down]

Select the next frame in the story

Windows [Ctrl]-[Alt]-[Shift]-[Page Up], *Mac* [⌘]-[Option]-[Shift]-[Page Up]

Select the first frame in the story

Windows [Ctrl]-[Alt]-[Shift]-[Page Down], *Mac* [⌘]-[Option]-[Shift]-[Page Down]

Select the last frame in the story

Keyboard Shortcuts for Duplicating Objects

Windows [Ctrl]-[Alt]-[Shift]-[D], *Mac* [⌘]-[Option]-[Shift]-[D]

Duplicate the selected object

Windows [Ctrl]-[Shift]-[V], *Mac* [⌘]-[Shift]-[V]

Display the Step And Repeat dialog box

After duplicating an object, press this shortcut to display the Step And Repeat dialog box (the Windows version is shown here). Use the controls to specify how many duplicates you want to create and the horizontal and vertical offsets to use, and then press Enter (on Windows) or Return (on the Mac).

Step and Repeat

Repeat Count: 24

Horizontal Offset: 1p6

Vertical Offset: 1p6

OK

Cancel

Windows Alt-drag, *Mac* Option-drag

Duplicate the selection

This shortcut works when the Selection tool, the Direct Selection tool, or the Group Selection tool is selected. Press Shift if you want to constrain the movement to 45-degree angles instead of moving freely.

» *Tip:* *To duplicate and transform a selection, Alt-drag it (on Windows) or Option-drag it (on the Mac) using a transformation tool.*

Windows Alt-←, Alt-→, Alt-↑, Alt-↓,
Mac Option-←, Option-→, Option-↑, Option-↓

Duplicate the selection and move it left, right, up, or down by one increment

For this shortcut and the next, InDesign uses the increment set in the Cursor Key text box on the Units & Increments sheet of the Preferences dialog box (Ctrl-K on Windows, ⌘-K on the Mac).

Windows Alt-Shift-←, Alt-Shift-→, Alt-Shift-↑, Alt-Shift-↓,
Mac Option-Shift-←, Option-Shift-→, Option-Shift-↑,
Option-Shift-↓

Duplicate the selection and move it left, right, up, or down by ten increments

Keyboard Shortcuts for Moving Objects

Windows ←, →, ↑, ↓, *Mac* ←, →, ↑, ↓

Move the selection by one increment

For this shortcut and the next, InDesign uses the increment set in the Cursor Key text box on the Units & Increments sheet of the Preferences dialog box (Ctrl-K on Windows, ⌘-K on the Mac).

Windows Shift-←, Shift-→, Shift-↑, Shift-↓,
Mac Shift-←, Shift-→, Shift-↑, Shift-↓

Move the selection by ten increments

Keyboard Shortcuts for Arranging Objects

Windows Ctrl-], *Mac* ⌘-]

Bring the selected object forward

Windows Ctrl-[, *Mac* ⌘-[

Send the selected object backward

Windows Ctrl-Shift-], *Mac* ⌘-Shift-]

Bring the selected object to the front

Windows Ctrl-Shift-[, *Mac* ⌘-Shift-[

Send the selected object to the back

Keyboard Shortcuts for Grouping Objects

Windows Ctrl-G, *Mac* ⌘-G

Group the selected objects

Windows Ctrl-Shift-G, *Mac* ⌘-Shift-G

Ungroup the selected group

Keyboard Shortcuts for Locking and Unlocking Objects

Windows Ctrl-L, *Mac* ⌘-L

Lock the position of the selected object or objects

Windows Ctrl-Alt-L, *Mac* ⌘-Option-L

Unlock the selected locked object or objects

InDesign

Keyboard Shortcuts for Working with Frames

Windows [Ctrl]-[B], *Mac* [⌘]-[B]

Display the Text Frame Options dialog box

Windows [Ctrl]-[Alt]-[E], *Mac* [⌘]-[Option]-[E]

Fit the content to the frame that contains it

When you press this shortcut, InDesign changes the content's proportions if necessary to match those of the frame.

Windows [Ctrl]-[Alt]-[C], *Mac* [⌘]-[Option]-[C]

Fit the frame to its contents

Windows [Ctrl]-[Shift]-[E], *Mac* [⌘]-[Shift]-[E]

Center the content within the frame

Windows [Ctrl]-[Alt]-[Shift]-[E], *Mac* [⌘]-[Option]-[Shift]-[E]

Fit the content to the frame, preserving the content's proportions

Windows [Shift]-drag with Selection tool, *Mac* [Shift]-drag with Selection tool

Resize the frame and its contents proportionally

Windows [Ctrl]-drag with Selection tool, *Mac* [⌘]-drag with Selection tool

Resize the frame and its contents

Keyboard Shortcuts for Drop Shadows and Paths

Windows [Ctrl]-[Alt]-[M], *Mac* [⌘]-[Option]-[M]

Display the Drop Shadow dialog box

Windows [Ctrl]-[Alt]-[Shift]-[K], *Mac* [⌘]-[Option]-[Shift]-[K]

Display the Clipping Path dialog box

Windows [Ctrl]-[8], *Mac* [⌘]-[8]

Make a compound path from the selected paths

Working with Tables

InDesign provides keyboard shortcuts for navigating in tables, displaying the dialog boxes for configuring tables, changing rows and columns, and selecting items in tables.

Keyboard Shortcuts for Navigating in Tables

Windows Tab , *Mac* Tab
  Move to the next cell

Windows Shift - Tab , *Mac* Shift - Tab
  Move to the previous cell

Windows ← , *Mac* ←
  Move left one cell

Windows → , *Mac* →
  Move right one cell

Windows ↑ , *Mac* ↑
  Move up one cell

Windows ↓ , *Mac* ↓
  Move down one cell

Windows Alt - Page Up , *Mac* Option - Page Up
  Move to the first cell in the column

Windows Alt - Page Down , *Mac* Option - Page Down
  Move to the last cell in the column

Windows Alt - Home , *Mac* Option - Home
  Move to the first cell in the row

Windows Alt - End , *Mac* Option - End
  Move to the last cell in the row

Windows [Page Up], *Mac* [Page Up]

Move to the first row in the frame

Windows [Page Down], *Mac* [Page Down]

Move to the last row in the frame

Keyboard Shortcuts for Choosing Options in Tables

Windows [Ctrl]-[Alt]-[Shift]-[T], *Mac* [⌘]-[Option]-[Shift]-[T]

Display the Insert Table dialog box

Define a text box, make the text cursor active in it, and then press this shortcut to display the Insert Table dialog box (the Mac version is shown here). Specify the number of rows, columns, header rows, and footer rows for the table, and then press [Enter] (on Windows) or [Return] (on the Mac).

Windows [Ctrl]-[Alt]-[Shift]-[B], *Mac* [⌘]-[Option]-[Shift]-[B]

Display the Table Options dialog box

InDesign displays the Table Setup tab or Table Setup sheet of the Table Options dialog box.

Windows [Ctrl]-[Alt]-[B], *Mac* [⌘]-[Option]-[B]

Display the Cell Options dialog box

InDesign displays the Text tab or Text sheet of the Cell Options dialog box.

Keyboard Shortcuts for Changing Rows and Columns

Windows [Ctrl]-[9], *Mac* [⌘]-[9]

Display the Insert Rows dialog box

Windows [Ctrl]-[Alt]-[9], *Mac* [⌘]-[Option]-[9]

Display the Insert Columns dialog box

Windows [Ctrl]-[Backspace], *Mac* [⌘]-[Delete]

Delete the active row

Windows ⌈Ctrl⌉-⌈Backspace⌉, *Mac* ⌈Shift⌉-⌈Delete⌉

Delete the active column

Windows ⌈Alt⌉-drag, *Mac* ⌈Option⌉-drag

Insert or delete rows or columns when dragging

Start dragging the row or column border as if to change the column width or the row height, and then hold down ⌈Alt⌉ or ⌈Option⌉ to make InDesign insert or delete rows or columns (as appropriate) instead.

Windows ⌈Shift⌉-drag, *Mac* ⌈Shift⌉-drag

Resize the rows or columns without changing the size of the table

Hold down ⌈Shift⌉ as you drag an interior row border or column border.

Windows ⌈Shift⌉-drag, *Mac* ⌈Shift⌉-drag

Resize the rows or columns proportionally

Hold down ⌈Shift⌉ as you drag the right table border or bottom table border.

Windows ⌈Enter⌉ on the numeric keypad, *Mac* ⌈Enter⌉ on the numeric keypad

Start a row on the next column

Windows ⌈Shift⌉-⌈Enter⌉ on the numeric keypad, *Mac* ⌈Shift⌉-⌈Enter⌉ on the numeric keypad

Start a row in the next frame

Keyboard Shortcuts for Selecting Table Items

Windows ⌈Esc⌉, *Mac* ⌈Esc⌉

Toggle between selecting text and selecting cells

Windows ⌈Ctrl⌉-⌈/⌉, *Mac* ⌈⌘⌉-⌈/⌉

Select the active cell

Windows ⌈Shift⌉-⌈↑⌉, *Mac* ⌈Shift⌉-⌈↑⌉

Select the cell above the active cell

Windows ⌈Shift⌉-⌈↓⌉, *Mac* ⌈Shift⌉-⌈↓⌉

Select the cell below the active cell

Windows Shift-←, *Mac* Shift-←

Select the cell to the left of the active cell

Windows Shift-→, *Mac* Shift-→

Select the cell to the right of the active cell

Windows Ctrl-3, *Mac* ⌘-3

Select the active row

Windows Ctrl-Alt-3, *Mac* ⌘-Option-3

Select the active column

Windows Ctrl-Alt-A, *Mac* ⌘-Option-A

Select the active table

Selecting Tools

This section lists the keyboard shortcuts for selecting tools in the Tools palette and the shortcuts for manipulating all palettes.

Keyboard Shortcuts for Selecting Tools

Windows W, *Mac* W

Toggle between Normal view and Preview

Windows V, *Mac* V

Select the Selection tool

Windows A, *Mac* A

Select the Direct Selection tool

Windows Ctrl-Tab, *Mac* ⌘-Ctrl-Tab

Toggle between the Selection tool and the Direct Selection tool

Windows Ctrl, *Mac* ⌘

Temporarily select the Selection tool or the Direct Selection tool

Pressing this shortcut selects whichever was last used of the Selection tool or the Direct Selection tool. This shortcut works when any tool other than a selection tool is selected.

Windows [Alt] and Direct Selection tool, *Mac* [Option] and Direct Selection tool

Temporarily select the Group Selection tool

Windows [Ctrl]-[Alt], *Mac* [⌘]-[Option]

Temporarily select the Group Selection tool

This shortcut works when the Pen tool, the Add Anchor Point tool, or the Delete Anchor Point tool is selected.

Windows [P], *Mac* [P]

Select the Pen tool

Windows [Shift] and Pen tool, *Mac* [Shift] and Pen tool

Keep the Pen tool selected

Press [Shift] to keep the Pen tool selected when the mouse pointer is over an anchor point or a path.

Windows [=], *Mac* [=]

Select the Add Anchor Point tool

Windows [Alt] and Scissors tool, *Mac* [Option] and Scissors tool

Temporarily select the Add Anchor Point tool

Windows [-], *Mac* [-]

Select the Delete Anchor Point tool

Windows [Alt], *Mac* [Option]

Temporarily switch between the Add Anchor Point tool and the Delete Anchor Point tool

Windows [Shift]-[C], *Mac* [Shift]-[C]

Select the Convert Direction Point tool

Windows Ctrl-Alt, *Mac* ⌘-Option

Temporarily select the Convert Direction Point tool

This shortcut works when the Direct Selection tool is selected.

Windows Alt, *Mac* Option

Temporarily select the Convert Direction Point tool

This shortcut works when the Pen tool is selected.

Windows T, *Mac* T

Select the Type tool

Windows Shift-T, *Mac* Shift-T

Select the Type On A Path tool

Windows N, *Mac* N

Select the Pencil tool

Windows \, *Mac* \

Select the Line tool

Windows F, *Mac* F

Select the Rectangle Frame tool

Windows M, *Mac* M

Select the Rectangle tool

Windows L, *Mac* L

Select the Ellipse tool

Windows R, *Mac* R

Select the Rotate tool

Windows S, *Mac* S

Select the Scale tool

Windows [O], *Mac* [O]

> *Select the Shear tool*

Windows [E], *Mac* [E]

> *Select the Free Transform tool*

Windows [I], *Mac* [I]

> *Select the Eyedropper tool*

Windows [K], *Mac* [K]

> *Select the Measure tool*

Windows [G], *Mac* [G]

> *Select the Gradient tool*

Windows [B], *Mac* [B]

> *Select the Button tool*

Windows [C], *Mac* [C]

> *Select the Scissors tool*

Windows [H], *Mac* [H]

> *Select the Hand tool*

Windows [Alt]-[Spacebar], *Mac* [Option]-[Spacebar]

> *Temporarily select the Hand tool*
>
> This shortcut works in both Layout mode and Text mode. In Layout mode, you can also press [Spacebar] (on both Windows and Mac) to temporarily select the Hand tool. In Text mode, you can also press [Alt] (on Windows) or [Option] (on the Mac) to temporarily select the Hand tool.

Windows [Z], *Mac* [Z]

> *Select the Zoom tool*

Windows [Ctrl]-[Spacebar], *Mac* [⌘]-[Spacebar]

> *Temporarily select the Zoom In tool*

Windows X, *Mac* X

Toggle between Fill and Stroke

Windows Shift-X, *Mac* Shift-X

Swap Fill and Stroke

Windows J, *Mac* J

Toggle between Formatting Affects Text and Formatting Affects Container

Windows , *Mac* ,

Apply color

Windows . , *Mac* .

Apply gradient

Windows / , *Mac* /

Apply no color

Keyboard Shortcuts for Working with Palettes

Windows Alt-click the Trash button, *Mac* Option-click the Trash button

Delete the object without confirmation

Windows Alt-click the New button, *Mac* Option-click the New button

Create a new item and display the dialog box for setting options for the item

Windows Shift-Enter, *Mac* Shift-Return

Apply the value in a field but keep the focus on the field

Windows Tab, *Mac* Tab

Apply the value to a field and select the next field

Pressing Tab has this effect only when the focus is in a palette.

Windows Ctrl-Alt-~, *Mac* ⌘-Option-~

Select the last option you used in the last palette you used

Windows Tab , *Mac* Tab

> *Toggle the display of all palettes, the Toolbox, and the Control palette*
>
> This shortcut works when there's no insertion point.

Windows Shift - Tab , *Mac* Shift - Tab

> *Toggle the display of all palettes except the Toolbox and the Control palette*
>
> This shortcut works when there's no insertion point.

Windows Ctrl - Alt - Tab , *Mac* ⌘ - Option - Tab

> *Open or close all stashed palettes*

Customizing Keyboard Shortcuts

As you've seen in this chapter, InDesign lets you perform a wide variety of maneuvers and invoke many commands by using keyboard shortcuts. But if you find particular keyboard shortcuts difficult to remember or to press, or if you want to use keyboard shortcuts for other commands, you can customize the keyboard shortcuts by working in the Keyboard Shortcuts dialog box. InDesign even lets you specify the context for each keyboard shortcut, so that you can use the same shortcut to perform different actions in different contexts. For example, you might create a shortcut that performed one action in text and another action in tables.

To customize keyboard shortcuts, follow these steps:

1. Choose Edit | Keyboard Shortcuts to display the Keyboard Shortcuts dialog box.

2. In the Set drop-down list, choose the set of shortcuts that you want to customize:

   - InDesign starts you off with a default set of shortcuts (named Default) and a set for QuarkXPress 4.0 (named Shortcuts For QuarkXPress 4.0).

   - You can create a new set of shortcuts by clicking the New Set button, entering the name in the New Set dialog box (the Mac version is shown here), and then pressing Enter (on Windows) or Return (on the Mac):

- You can delete a set of shortcuts by selecting it in the Set drop-down list, clicking the Delete Set button, and then clicking the Yes button in the confirmation message box.

- To see at a glance which shortcuts the selected set includes, click the Show Set button. InDesign exports the shortcuts to a text file and displays it in Notepad (on Windows) or TextEdit (on the Mac). InDesign saves the text file under the name of the set of shortcuts—for example, Default.txt for the default set, or ShortcutsforQuarkXPress4.0.txt for the Shortcuts For QuarkXPress 4.0 set. In Windows, InDesign saves the text file in your My Documents folder. On Mac OS X, InDesign saves the text file in the Applications/Adobe InDesign CS/Presets/InDesign Shortcut Sets folder, so you have to dig a bit further before you can delete it.

3. In the Product Area drop-down list, select the category you want to work with so that InDesign displays its commands in the Commands list box. This drop-down list contains an item for each menu (for example, the Object Menu item contains the commands associated with the Object menu), a Tools item for tools, and descriptive items for other commands. If you can't find the command you're looking for, try the Other category.

4. In the Commands list box, select the command you want to customize. InDesign displays any shortcuts assigned to the command in the Current Shortcuts text box, together with the context in which it applies—for example, Default-Opt+Page Up for a shortcut that applies in the default context, or Text-Ctrl+Down Arrow for a shortcut that applies in the text context.

5. In the Context drop-down list, specify the context for the keyboard shortcut: Alerts, Dialogs (in message boxes and dialog boxes); Text (in text); Default; Tables (in tables); or XML Selection (in an XML selection).

6. Click in the New Shortcut text box.

7. Press the shortcut you want to use for the command.

8. Click the Assign button.

9. To remove an existing shortcut, select it in the Current Shortcuts list box, and then click the Remove button.

10. After you finish customizing shortcuts, click the Save button to save your changes.

11. Click the OK button to close the Keyboard Shortcuts dialog box.

GoLive Keyboard Shortcuts

Like the other applications in Creative Suite, GoLive offers plenty of keyboard shortcuts for operations you'll need to perform frequently, from basic operations such as creating and saving files to working in Links view and Navigation view. You can also customize GoLive's default keyboard shortcuts with shortcuts of your own.

First, one general point: GoLive has more variation between Windows shortcuts and Mac shortcuts than the other Creative Suite applications, so don't be surprised when one platform uses a different letter than the other for a particular shortcut— or when one platform has a shortcut that the other doesn't have at all.

Creating, Opening, Saving, and Closing Files

This section details the keyboard shortcuts that GoLive offers for creating pages, folders, and sites; opening, closing, and saving files; page setup, printing, and preview; configuring GoLive; and hiding and quitting the application.

Keyboard Shortcuts for Creating Items

Windows Ctrl-N, *Mac* ⌘-N

Create a new blank page

Windows Ctrl-Alt-Shift-N, *Mac* ⌘-Option-N

Launch the GoLive Site Wizard

Follow the wizard's screens to create a new web site.

Windows Ctrl-Alt-Shift-T, *Mac* ⌘-Option-Shift-N

Display the Select Template dialog box

In the Select Template dialog box, select the template to use for the new page you want to create.

Windows `Ctrl`-`Alt`-`Shift`-`F`, *Mac* `⌘`-`Option`-`Shift`-`F`

Create a new folder

Keyboard Shortcuts for Opening and Closing Files

Windows `Ctrl`-`O`, *Mac* `⌘`-`O`

Display the Open dialog box

Mac `⌘`-`Option`-`N`

Open the most recently used site

Press `⌘`-`Option` and the number of the most recently used site. For example, press `⌘`-`Option`-`1` to open the last site or `⌘`-`Option`-`2` to open the second-to-last site.

Windows `Ctrl`-`Shift`-`O`, *Mac* `⌘`-`Shift`-`O`

Display the Download Page dialog box

In the Download Page dialog box (the Mac version is shown here), specify the URL of the page to download. Click the Save As button to display the Save: GoLive dialog box, specify the filename and location, and then click the Save button.

Windows `Ctrl`-`W`, *Mac* `⌘`-`W`

Close the active file

Keyboard Shortcuts for Saving Files

Windows `Ctrl`-`S`, *Mac* `⌘`-`S`

Save the active file

The first time you save a file, GoLive displays the Save As dialog box so that you can specify the filename, the folder, and the format to use. Thereafter, when you issue a Save command, GoLive saves the file under its existing name without displaying the Save As dialog box.

Windows Ctrl-Shift-S, *Mac* ⌘-Shift-S

Display the Save As dialog box

Use the Save As dialog box to save a file under a different name, in a different location, or both.

Windows Ctrl-E, *Mac* ⌘-E

Display the Export Site Options dialog box

In the Export Site Options dialog box (the Windows version is shown here), choose options for exporting the site, and then click the Export button to display the Create A Site Folder dialog box.

Keyboard Shortcuts for Page Setup, Printing, and Preview

Windows Ctrl-Shift-P, *Mac* ⌘-Shift-P

Display the Page Setup dialog box

Windows Ctrl-P, *Mac* ⌘-P

Display the Print dialog box

Windows Ctrl-T, *Mac* ⌘-T

Preview in GoLive's Live Rendering window

Windows Ctrl-Shift-T, *Mac* ⌘-Shift-T

Preview in your default browser

The default browser is the browser specified on the Browsers sheet of the Preferences dialog box (Ctrl-K in Windows, ⌘-K on the Mac). You can specify more than one default browser, which enables you to use this command to quickly check a page in all the browsers you need it to be compatible with on this platform.

Keyboard Shortcuts for Configuring GoLive

Windows Ctrl-K, *Mac* ⌘-K

Display the Preferences dialog box

Windows Ctrl-Shift-K, *Mac* ⌘-Shift-K

Display the Web Settings dialog box

Windows Ctrl-Alt-Shift-K, *Mac* ⌘-Option-Shift-K

Display the Keyboard Shortcuts dialog box

See "Customizing Keyboard Shortcuts," at the end of this chapter, for a discussion of how to customize keyboard shortcuts in GoLive.

Keyboard Shortcuts for Hiding and Quitting

Mac ⌘-H

Hide GoLive

Mac ⌘-Option-H

Hide all other applications except GoLive

Windows Alt-F4, Ctrl-Q, *Mac* ⌘-Q

Quit GoLive

Performing Standard Editing Operations

In addition to shortcuts for undoing and redoing actions, GoLive lets you revert to the last saved version of a file so that you can quickly undo the changes you've made. GoLive also offers shortcuts for other standard editing operations such as Cut, Copy, and Paste; selecting items; finding and replacing text; checking syntax and spelling; and moving boxes.

Keyboard Shortcuts for Undo, Redo, and Revert To Saved

Windows Ctrl-Z, *Mac* ⌘-Z

Undo the last command

Windows [Ctrl]-[Shift]-[Z], *Mac* [⌘]-[Shift]-[Z]

Redo the last command you undid

Windows [Ctrl]-[Alt]-[Shift]-[Z], *Mac* [⌘]-[Option]-[Z]

Revert to the last saved version of the active file

Press this shortcut and click the Yes button (in Windows) or the OK button (on the Mac) in the resulting dialog box (the Mac version is shown here) to discard the changes you've made since last saving the file. Reverting to the last saved version has the same effect as closing the file without saving changes, and then reopening it, but is faster and easier.

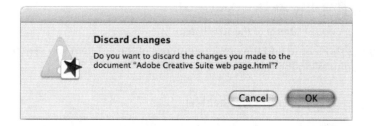

Keyboard Shortcuts for Cut, Copy, and Paste

Windows [Ctrl]-[X], *Mac* [⌘]-[X]

Cut

Windows [Ctrl]-[C], *Mac* [⌘]-[C]

Copy

Windows [Ctrl]-[V], *Mac* [⌘]-[V]

Paste

Windows [Ctrl]-[D], *Mac* [⌘]-[D]

Duplicate

Use the Duplicate command to copy objects, their connectors, and their links.

Keyboard Shortcuts for Selecting Items

Windows [Ctrl]-[A], *Mac* [⌘]-[A]

Select all items

Keyboard Shortcuts for Find and Replace

Windows Ctrl-F, *Mac* ⌘-F

Display the Find Content window

Windows Ctrl-G, *Mac* ⌘-G

Find the next instance of the search item

Press this shortcut to find the next instance of the last item you searched for, without displaying the Find Content window.

Windows Ctrl-Alt-G, *Mac* ⌘-Option-G

Find the previous instance of the search item

Press this shortcut to find the previous instance of the last item you searched for, without displaying the Find Content window.

Windows Ctrl-Shift-H, *Mac* ⌘-Shift-H

Find the next instance of the current selection

Windows Ctrl-Alt-R, *Mac* ⌘-Option-R

Replace the selection with the contents of the Replace text box

Windows Ctrl-Alt-Shift-H, *Mac* ⌘-Option-Shift-R

Replace the selection and find the next instance

Press this shortcut to replace the selection with the contents of the Replace text box in the Find Content window and find the next instance of the search item.

Keyboard Shortcuts for Checking Spelling and Syntax

Windows Ctrl-Shift-U, *Mac* ⌘-Option-U

Display the Check Spelling dialog box

Windows Ctrl-Alt-Shift-B, *Mac* ⌘-Option-K

Display the Syntax Check dialog box for checking web coding syntax

Keyboard Shortcuts for Moving Boxes

Windows [Ctrl]-[Alt]-[←], [Ctrl]-[Alt]-[→], [Ctrl]-[Alt]-[↑], [Ctrl]-[Alt]-[↓],
Mac [Option]-[←], [Option]-[→], [Option]-[↑], [Option]-[↓]

Move the selected box in the layout grid by pixel

Windows [←], [→], [↑], [↓], *Mac* [←], [→], [↑], [↓]

Move the selected box based on the Snap To Grid setting

Changing the View and Displaying Items

This section lists the keyboard shortcuts that GoLive offers for zooming the view; displaying and hiding items; displaying the CSS Editor, DHTML Timeline Editor, and the JavaScript Editor; displaying and hiding windows; and displaying and hiding palettes.

Keyboard Shortcuts for Zooming the View

Windows [Ctrl]-[+], *Mac* [⌘]-[+]

Zoom in

This shortcut and the next work less consistently on Windows than on the Mac. You can use the zoom buttons on the status bar instead if necessary.

Windows [Ctrl]-[-], *Mac* [⌘]-[-]

Zoom out

Keyboard Shortcuts for Displaying and Hiding Items

Windows [Ctrl]-[Alt]-[Shift]-[E], *Mac* [⌘]-[Option]-[E]

View the document's source code

Windows [Ctrl]-[Y], *Mac* [⌘]-[Y]

Toggle splitting on the window, displaying source code in the lower part

Windows [Ctrl]-[Shift]-[D], *Mac* [⌘]-[Shift]-[D]

Refresh the layout

Windows [Ctrl]-[Shift]-[I], *Mac* [⌘]-[Shift]-[I]

Toggle the display of invisible items

Windows [Ctrl]-[Alt]-[Shift]-[W], *Mac* [⌘]-[Option]-[Shift]-[L]

Toggle the display of link warnings

Windows [Ctrl]-[R], *Mac* [⌘]-[R]

Toggle the display of the rulers

Keyboard Shortcuts for Displaying the CSS, DHTML, and JavaScript Editors

Windows [Ctrl]-[Alt]-[Shift]-[C], *Mac* [⌘]-[Option]-[C]

Display the CSS Editor window

Windows [Ctrl]-[Alt]-[Shift]-[D], *Mac* [⌘]-[Option]-[Shift]-[D]

Display the DHTML Timeline Editor window

Windows [Ctrl]-[Shift]-[J], *Mac* [⌘]-[Option]-[J]

Display the JavaScript Editor window

Keyboard Shortcuts for Displaying and Hiding Windows

Windows [Ctrl]-[F6], [Ctrl]-[Tab]

Display the next window

Windows [Ctrl]-[Shift]-[F6], [Ctrl]-[Shift]-[Tab]

Display the previous window

Windows [Alt]-[-], then [N], *Mac* [⌘]-[M]

Minimize the active window

Windows [Ctrl]-[J], *Mac* [⌘]-[J]

Hide or redisplay all displayed palettes

Windows Ctrl - O

Toggle the display of the main toolbar

Windows Ctrl - Shift - O

Toggle the display of the Version Cue toolbar

Keyboard Shortcuts for Displaying and Hiding Palettes

The following keyboard shortcuts let you quickly activate, display, and hide the palettes you need. When a palette has only one tab, the keyboard shortcut acts as a toggle: if the palette is displayed, pressing the shortcut hides the palette; and if the palette is hidden, pressing the shortcut displays it. When a palette has multiple tabs, pressing the keyboard shortcut:

- Displays the palette if it's hidden

- Activates the palette if it's displayed but one of the other tabs is active

- Hides the palette if it's displayed and active

>> Note: *In Windows, the Highlight palette, the History palette, and the In & Out Links palette are separate palettes, whereas on the Mac these palettes are combined with other palettes. So in Windows, the keyboard shortcuts for these palettes simply toggle the display of the palettes.*

Windows Ctrl - 2 , *Mac* ⌘ - 2

Toggle the display of the Objects palette

Mac ⌘ - 8

Activate or toggle the display of the Align palette

Windows Ctrl - Shift - 9 , *Mac* ⌘ - Option - 9

Activate or toggle the display of the CSS palette

Windows Ctrl - 3 , *Mac* ⌘ - 3

Activate or toggle the display of the Color palette

Windows Ctrl - Shift - 4 , *Mac* ⌘ - Option - 4

Activate or toggle the display of the Highlight palette

Windows Ctrl - 7 , *Mac* ⌘ - 7

Activate or toggle the display of the History palette

Windows `Ctrl`-`5`, *Mac* `⌘`-`5`

  Activate or toggle the display of the In & Out Links palette

Windows `Ctrl`-`1`, *Mac* `⌘`-`1`

  Activate or toggle the display of the Inspector palette

Windows `Ctrl`-`4`, *Mac* `⌘`-`4`

  Activate or toggle the display of the Layers palette

Windows `Ctrl`-`Shift`-`7`, *Mac* `⌘`-`Option`-`7`

  Toggle the display of the Rollovers & Actions palette

Windows `Ctrl`-`6`, *Mac* `⌘`-`6`

  Activate or toggle the display of the Table palette

Windows `Ctrl`-`Shift`-`6`, *Mac* `⌘`-`Option`-`6`

  Activate or toggle the display of the Tracing Image palette

Windows `Ctrl`-`Shift`-`5`, *Mac* `⌘`-`Option`-`5`

  Activate or toggle the display of the Transform palette

Windows `Ctrl`-`9`, *Mac* `⌘`-`9`

  Activate or toggle the display of the View palette

Working with Text, Type, and Source Code

This section details GoLive's keyboard shortcuts for the following:

- Navigating in text, and selecting text
- Inserting items (such as line breaks and nonbreaking spaces)
- Working with type
- Applying character formatting, paragraph formatting, and alignment
- Working with tags
- Using the DHTML timeline
- Working with tables in Layout view

Keyboard Shortcuts for Navigating in Text

You can use these shortcuts for navigating in both text and source code.

Windows [Ctrl]-[←], *Mac* [Option]-[←]

Move the cursor to the beginning of the current word

Windows [Ctrl]-[→], *Mac* [Option]-[→]

Move the cursor to the end of the current word

Windows [Home], *Mac* [⌘]-[←]

Move the cursor to the beginning of the line

Windows [End], *Mac* [⌘]-[→]

Move the cursor to the end of the line

Windows [Ctrl]-[↑], *Mac* [⌘]-[↑]

Move the cursor to the start of the document

Windows [Ctrl]-[↓], *Mac* [⌘]-[↓]

Move the cursor to the end of the document

Keyboard Shortcuts for Selecting Text

You can use these shortcuts for selecting both text and source code.

Windows [Shift]-[←], *Mac* [Shift]-[←]

Select one character to the left

Windows [Shift]-[→], *Mac* [Shift]-[→]

Select one character to the right

Windows [Shift]-[↑], *Mac* [Shift]-[↑]

Select one line up

Windows [Shift]-[↓], *Mac* [Shift]-[↓]

Select one line down

GoLive

Windows Shift-Home, *Mac* ⌘-Shift-←

Select from the cursor to the beginning of the line

Windows Shift-End, *Mac* ⌘-Shift-→

Select from the cursor to the end of the line

Windows Ctrl-Shift-↑, *Mac* ⌘-Shift-↑

Select from the cursor to the start of the document

Windows Ctrl-Shift-↓, *Mac* ⌘-Shift-↓

Select from the cursor to the end of the document

Keyboard Shortcuts for Inserting Items

Windows Shift-Enter, *Mac* Shift-Return

Insert a line break

Windows Shift-Spacebar, *Mac* Option-Spacebar

Insert a nonbreaking space

Windows Ctrl--

Insert a word-break tag (<WBR>)

Keyboard Shortcuts for Working with Type

Windows Ctrl-Alt-Shift-G, *Mac* ⌘-Option-F

Display the Font Editor dialog box

Windows Ctrl-Alt-Shift-U, *Mac* ⌘-Option-Shift-U

Apply default unnumbered list formatting

Keyboard Shortcuts for Applying Character Formatting

Windows Ctrl-Shift-N, *Mac* ⌘-Shift-N

Apply plain text formatting

Windows [Ctrl]-[B], *Mac* [⌘]-[B]

Toggle boldface

Windows [Ctrl]-[I], *Mac* [⌘]-[I]

Toggle italic

Windows [Ctrl]-[U], *Mac* [⌘]-[U]

Toggle underline

Windows [Ctrl]-[Alt]-[Shift]-[7], *Mac* [⌘]-[Option]-[Shift]-[7]

Toggle strikethrough

Keyboard Shortcuts for Applying Paragraph Formatting

Windows [Ctrl]-[Alt]-[Shift]-[0], *Mac* [⌘]-[Option]-[Shift]-[P]

Apply Normal style

Windows [Ctrl]-[Alt]-[Shift]-[1], *Mac* [⌘]-[Option]-[Shift]-[1]

Apply Heading 1 style

Windows [Ctrl]-[Alt]-[Shift]-[2], *Mac* [⌘]-[Option]-[Shift]-[2]

Apply Heading 2 style

Windows [Ctrl]-[Alt]-[Shift]-[3], *Mac* [⌘]-[Option]-[Shift]-[3]

Apply Heading 3 style

Windows [Ctrl]-[Alt]-[Shift]-[4], *Mac* [⌘]-[Option]-[Shift]-[4]

Apply Heading 4 style

Windows [Ctrl]-[Alt]-[Shift]-[5], *Mac* [⌘]-[Option]-[Shift]-[5]

Apply Heading 5 style

Windows [Ctrl]-[Alt]-[Shift]-[6], *Mac* [⌘]-[Option]-[Shift]-[6]

Apply Heading 6 style

GoLive

Keyboard Shortcuts for Applying Alignment

Windows `Ctrl`-`Shift`-`L`, *Mac* `⌘`-`Shift`-`L`

Align left

Windows `Ctrl`-`Shift`-`C`, *Mac* `⌘`-`Shift`-`C`

Center

Windows `Ctrl`-`Shift`-`R`, *Mac* `⌘`-`Shift`-`R`

Align right

Keyboard Shortcuts for Working with Tags

Windows `Tab`, *Mac* `Tab`

Select the next text box

Windows `Shift`-`Tab`, *Mac* `Shift`-`Tab`

Select the previous text box

Windows `Ctrl`-click a tag name, *Mac* `⌘`-click a tag name

Display the tag shortcut menu

Windows `Enter` on the numeric keypad, *Mac* `Return`

Expand or collapse the selected tag

Windows `Shift`-`Enter` on the numeric keypad, *Mac* `Option`-`Return`

Recursively expand or collapse the selected tag

Keyboard Shortcuts for Using the DHTML Timeline

Windows `←`, *Mac* `←`

Select the previous keyframe

Windows `→`, *Mac* `→`

Select the next keyframe

Windows ⬆, *Mac* ⬆

Select the previous track

Windows ⬇, *Mac* ⬇

Select the next track

Windows Enter on the numeric keypad, *Mac* Enter on the numeric keypad

Play the scene from the position of the time cursor

Windows 0 on the numeric keypad, *Mac* 0 on the numeric keypad

Stop the playback of the scene

Windows Ctrl-click a time track, *Mac* ⌘-click a time track

Create a new keyframe

Windows Alt-drag a keyframe, *Mac* Option-drag a keyframe

Duplicate the keyframe

Windows Ctrl-click an action, *Mac* ⌘-click an action

Create an action placeholder

Click the action on the action track.

Windows Ctrl-Shift-drag, *Mac* Ctrl-drag

Scale an animation

Keyboard Shortcuts for Working with Tables in Layout View

Windows Tab, *Mac* Tab

Move the cursor to the next cell

Windows Shift-Tab, *Mac* Shift-Tab

Move the cursor to the previous cell

Windows Ctrl-Enter, *Mac* Ctrl-Return

Change from text entry mode to cell selection mode

Windows Enter, *Mac* Return

Change from cell selection mode to text entry mode

Windows Alt-drag a border, *Mac* Option-drag a border

Change a row's height or a column's width

Windows Shift-click, *Mac* Shift-click

Select multiple noncontiguous cells

Click the first cell, then hold down Shift and click the cells you want to add to the selection.

Windows Ctrl-Shift-drag, *Mac* ⌘-drag

Add rows or columns as you drag

Press this shortcut and drag the right border or the bottom border of the table to add the rows or columns.

Windows *, *Mac* *

Add a row above the active row (in cell selection mode)

Windows +, *Mac* +

Add a column to the left of the active column (in cell selection mode)

Windows -, *Mac* -

Add a column to the right of the active column (in cell selection mode)

Windows Ctrl-Delete, *Mac* Backspace

Delete the active column (in cell selection mode)

Windows Shift-→, *Mac* Shift-→

Join the active cell with the cell to its right

Windows Shift-←, *Mac* Shift-←

Split the active cell into two cells vertically

This shortcut works only for cells that you've previously joined (for example, by using the previous shortcut).

Windows Shift-↓, *Mac* Shift-↓

Join the active cell with the cell below it

Windows [Shift]-[↑], *Mac* [Shift]-[↑]

Split the active cell into two cells horizontally

This shortcut works only for cells that you've previously joined (for example, by using the previous shortcut).

Performing Special Operations

This section explains GoLive's shortcuts for working with links and for performing "special" operations—everything from displaying the Visual Tag Editor dialog box to inserting text macros in your source code.

Keyboard Shortcuts for Working with Links

Windows [Ctrl]-[L], *Mac* [⌘]-[L]

Create a new link

Windows [Ctrl]-[Alt]-[Shift]-[L], *Mac* [⌘]-[Option]-[L]

Remove the selected link

Windows [Alt]-drag, *Mac* [⌘]-drag

Create a new link between the dragged item and its destination

Select the item you want to link, hold down [Alt] or [⌘], drag the item to its destination, and release it when GoLive applies a highlight to the destination.

Windows [Ctrl]-drag, *Mac* [⌘]-drag

Link the dragged frame to the page

Hold down [Ctrl] or [⌘] and drag the frame to the target page in the site window.

Keyboard Shortcuts for Performing Special Operations

Windows [Ctrl]-[Shift]-[E], *Mac* [⌘]-[Shift]-[E]

Display the Visual Tag Editor dialog box

Windows [Ctrl]-[Shift]-[A], *Mac* [⌘]-[Shift]-[A]

Add the selected word to the keywords list

Windows [Ctrl]-[Alt]-[Shift]-[J], *Mac* [⌘]-[Option]-[T]

Start setting the tab index order

Windows Ctrl-Shift-B, *Mac* ⌘-Shift-B

Issue a Select Upper Block command

The Select Upper Block command selects the parent HTML element of the selected element. The parent element is the element in the next level up the hierarchy that encloses the selected element.

Windows Ctrl-Shift-M, *Mac* ⌘-Shift-M

Insert the specified text macro in the source code

Type the name of the macro, and then press this shortcut to enter its contents. Text macros aren't case sensitive, so you can type the name in whichever case suits you.

Windows Ctrl-Alt-Shift-I, *Mac* ⌘-Option-Shift-I

Display the Document Statistics dialog box

Using Links View and Navigation View

Links view and Navigation view let you quickly check the arrangement of your sites and find the pages you need to work with. GoLive provides keyboard shortcuts for getting around quickly and easily in these views.

Keyboard Shortcuts for Links View and Navigation View

Windows ←, →, ↑, ↓, *Mac* ←, →, ↑, ↓

Select the next file in the direction of the arrow you press

Windows Ctrl-↑, *Mac* ⌘-↑

Start a partial tree from the selection

Windows Ctrl-↓, *Mac* ⌘-↓

Toggle the display of child elements of the selected parent element

Pressing this shortcut has the same effect as clicking the Expand button on a parent element.

Windows Shift-↑, *Mac* Shift-↑

Add the parent element to the selection

Windows Shift-↓, *Mac* Shift-↓

  Add the child elements to the selection

Windows Ctrl-←, *Mac* Option-←

  Select the previous sibling element

  If there is no previous sibling element, pressing this shortcut selects the nearest item to the left of the selected element.

Windows Ctrl-→, *Mac* Option-→

  Select the next sibling element

  If there is no next sibling element, pressing this shortcut selects the nearest item to the right of the selected element.

Windows Ctrl-↑, *Mac* Option-↑

  Select the closest element above the selected element

Windows Ctrl-↓, *Mac* Option-↓

  Select the closest element below the selected element

Windows Esc, *Mac* Esc

  Toggle the display of a partial tree from the selection, and move to the center

Windows Ctrl-Home, *Mac* ⌘-Home

  Select the top-level references

Windows Home, *Mac* Home

  Select the first sibling element

Windows End, *Mac* End

  Select the last sibling element

Windows Enter, *Mac* Enter

  Open the selected reference

Windows Spacebar, *Mac* Spacebar

  Temporarily display the Hand tool

GoLive

Press [Spacebar] to display the Hand tool, then drag to scroll the window.

Windows [Shift]-click, *Mac* [Option]-click

Toggle the zoom between 100 percent and 200 percent

Windows [Shift]-drag, *Mac* [Option]-drag

Zoom to fit the rectangle you select

Press [Shift] or [Option], drag to select the rectangle you want to see, and release the mouse button and the key to make GoLive zoom the display to show only the contents of that rectangle.

Customizing Keyboard Shortcuts

If GoLive's built-in keyboard shortcuts don't suit you, or if you need more shortcuts, you can customize them. GoLive offers less customization than some of the other Creative Suite applications: you can create a new shortcut for a menu command that doesn't have one, or replace the existing shortcut for a menu item, but that's all.

To customize keyboard shortcuts, follow these steps:

1. Display the Keyboard Shortcuts dialog box (the Windows version is shown here with customization under way):

   - In Windows, press [Ctrl]-[Alt]-[Shift]-[K] or choose Edit | Keyboard Shortcuts.
   - On the Mac, press [⌘]-[Option]-[Shift]-[K] or choose GoLive | Keyboard Shortcuts.

2. In the Selected Set drop-down list, choose the set of shortcuts you want to customize:

- GoLive starts you off with a set called GoLive Factory Defaults, which should be selected by default, and a set called GoLive 5 Set (for people used to GoLive 5).

- To create a new set, click the New Set button. GoLive displays the New Set dialog box (the Windows version is shown here). Enter the name for the new set in the Set Name text box. In the Copy From drop-down list, choose the existing set of shortcuts on which you want to base the new set. (To start with, you'll probably want to base the new set on the GoLive Factory Defaults set.) Then click the OK button. GoLive selects the new set in the Selected Set drop-down list.

New Set	✕
Set Name	Sharleen's Shortcuts
Copy From	GoLive Factory Defaults ⌄
	OK Cancel

- To delete a set of shortcuts, select it in the Selected Set drop-down list, click the Delete Set button, and then click the OK button in the confirmation dialog box.

3. In the list box, expand the menu category that contains the command you want to affect.

4. Select the command.

5. Click in the Press New Shortcut text box.

6. Press the keyboard shortcut you want to use for the command.

7. Check the Currently Assigned To box to see if the shortcut is currently assigned to another command. If so, decide whether to change it. (To change it, press another shortcut.)

8. Click the Assign button to assign the shortcut to the command. If the command already has a shortcut assigned, GoLive displays the Replace button in place of the Assign button. Click this button if you want to replace the existing shortcut.

9. When you've finished customizing keyboard shortcuts, click the OK button to close the Keyboard Shortcuts dialog box.

Index

INTERNATIONAL CONTACT INFORMATION

AUSTRALIA
McGraw-Hill Book Company
Australia Pty. Ltd.
TEL +61-2-9900-1800
FAX +61-2-9878-8881
http://www.mcgraw-hill.com.au
books-it_sydney@mcgraw-hill.com

CANADA
McGraw-Hill Ryerson Ltd.
TEL +905-430-5000
FAX +905-430-5020
http://www.mcgraw-hill.ca

**GREECE, MIDDLE EAST, & AFRICA
(Excluding South Africa)**
McGraw-Hill Hellas
TEL +30-210-6560-990
TEL +30-210-6560-993
TEL +30-210-6560-994
FAX +30-210-6545-525

MEXICO (Also serving Latin America)
McGraw-Hill Interamericana Editores
S.A. de C.V.
TEL +525-1500-5108
FAX +525-117-1589
http://www.mcgraw-hill.com.mx
carlos_ruiz@mcgraw-hill.com

SINGAPORE (Serving Asia)
McGraw-Hill Book Company
TEL +65-6863-1580
FAX +65-6862-3354
http://www.mcgraw-hill.com.sg
mghasia@mcgraw-hill.com

SOUTH AFRICA
McGraw-Hill South Africa
TEL +27-11-622-7512
FAX +27-11-622-9045
robyn_swanepoel@mcgraw-hill.com

SPAIN
McGraw-Hill/
Interamericana de España, S.A.U.
TEL +34-91-180-3000
FAX +34-91-372-8513
http://www.mcgraw-hill.es
professional@mcgraw-hill.es

**UNITED KINGDOM, NORTHERN,
EASTERN, & CENTRAL EUROPE**
McGraw-Hill Education Europe
TEL +44-1-628-502500
FAX +44-1-628-770224
http://www.mcgraw-hill.co.uk
emea_queries@mcgraw-hill.com

ALL OTHER INQUIRIES Contact:
McGraw-Hill/Osborne
TEL +1-510-420-7700
FAX +1-510-420-7703
http://www.osborne.com
omg_international@mcgraw-hill.com